MODERN NOMAD

MODERN NOMAD

THE VANLIFE ALTERNATIVE

GARY VARNER

OWLERY
PRESS

Editing and cover illustration by Micaleah Newman.
Cover and book layout by G. Lloyd.
Original poems and photos by the author.

Published by Owlery Press LLC.

ISBN 979-8-9864863-1-4

❀ Created with Vellum

To Dad, whose wanderlust genes eventually influenced me.

*When I was twenty-something, Dad bought a 33' motorhome.
I was a little embarrassed, silently vowed never to be an old fart
wandering around in an RV.*

Oops

CONTENTS

PREFACE

> Twenty years from now you will be more disappointed by the things that you didn't do than by the ones you did do. So throw off the bowlines. Sail away from the safe harbor. Catch the trade winds in your sails. Explore. Dream. Discover.
>
> MARK TWAIN

The dream of a wandering life, one filled with new horizons, open expectations, and fresh adventures, likely dates back to when humans began walking on two legs and roaming the earth. While many early humans were nomads by necessity, moving with the seasons or following food sources, I want to believe some experienced the pull of a human desire to wander for wandering's sake.

Some of us catch nomadic wanderlust and yearn to explore new horizons later in life, while the lucky ones do so earlier. Those who get the spark early often sacrifice to keep wandering, rather than settle on a 9-to-5 existence.

I knew this feeling most of my life, but as many did, never got beyond much more than infrequent vacations to sate my need. I know better now, and for the rest of my days I will continue traveling, a modern nomad seeking to learn and experience all I can while still able to put one foot in front of the other and rubber on the road.

This book came about after a long period of sharing my experiences with others, helping many through social media (especially in targeted Facebook groups) and in person, solve how to do this thing called vanlife. Throughout those years, I realized many people adopt vanlife without knowing what to do, which vehicle to get, or how to travel in this form. Many just extend what they do at home to what they do in their home on wheels. Thus, they learn the hard way that vanlife differs from houselife.

As I wrote the first draft of this book, I quickly realized how bottom-less this topic could be. Covering every aspect, or every newbie or experienced traveler's needs, could take years to write. My ultimate purpose in sharing what I learned and discovered is to help others make the jump into this amazing alternative lifestyle. *Modern Nomad: The Vanlife Alternative* is a guidebook to inform travelers of any experi-ence level on how to adopt or improve their vanlife, make better choices while avoiding mistakes, time-consuming detours, and unnec-essary expense. That is not to say rookie mistakes are not great learning opportunities; even experienced vanlifers still earn their share of such goofs.

From how to get started, to what to consider, and finally how to live vanlife with its varied options and challenges, *Modern Nomad: The Vanlife Alternative* can be the impetus you need to make vanlife happen for you. For many, this alternative lifestyle is a rebirth of sorts, a possible unburdening of baggage and unloading of things no longer needed to live a fulfilled life.

While much of the content here focuses on full-time vanlife, these guidelines and suggestions can apply to however you travel in vanlife.

See "Appendix D – Contact & Follow" for how to contact me if you have questions, are interested in a presentation on this topic to your group or class, or just want to say hi. Links are provided to follow my vanlife journey on my blog, Instagram, or my Adventures Nomadic YouTube channel.

I hope you find my thoughts, experiences, and guidance in this book helpful.

Best of luck on your vanlife journey!

NOMAD

Am I an ant
scurrying about,
seeking good food
to take underground?

Or am I an owl,
wise as they say,
patiently waiting,
for food to appear.

No, I am a snail,
traveling with shell,
slowly searching
for new tomorrows.

CHAPTER 1
LIVING THE DREAM

> Now more than ever do I realize that I will never be content with a sedentary life, that I will always be haunted by thoughts of a sun-drenched elsewhere.
>
> ISABELLE EBERHARDT

When I first told family and friends I planned to spend more time wandering in a van than living in a house, many replied, "I'm jealous! You're living the dream! I hope to do that someday."

To which I thought, but never asked, "Which dream is that? And what are you waiting for?"

OLD THINKING & NEW INFLUENCES

My parents' generation strove for that quintessential American Dream: buying a house and eventually paying it off and living free! Except "living free" never really arrives, because there are always taxes and upkeep, repairs and maintenance, and eventually remodeling updates. I doubt many members of the current workforce feel the same way about owning a house as my parents did. Social and economic conditions evolved to make such an achievement more challenging than ever before. The cost of housing today makes owning a home more like an impossible dream.

Becoming equally rare is the dream of retiring comfortably from a life of dedicated work, able to afford to relax, maybe travel, and of course, spoil the grandchildren. The dream of a comfortable life in one's elder years is unreachable by many. Per a CNBC report, roughly 46% of Americans carry debt into their retirement years. Many must continue to work, or find new work, plus the challenge of finding affordable housing. Those who have settled children might be able to live with them, while others may become a statistic in the growing homeless masses.

VANLIFE'S SOCIETAL & ECONOMIC ROOTS

A new alternative culture emerged to answer some of these challenges, and is increasing in numbers every year. People began living in their vehicles when traditional homes were no longer an option for them. Those who choose to live in a vehicle and move with the weather, rather than in homeless tent camps or shelters, have the benefit of living with dignity and a sense of self-reliance. While living in abandoned or disabled vehicles is nothing new, the option to live in a movable vehicle began in the western U.S. and spread elsewhere over the years. Vanlife is a lifestyle for people who chose to live in, or travel extensively in a small van or vehicle. For many, this lifestyle enables a life of freedom and affordability they needed or craved.

Some choose a car, others a remodeled school bus, or whatever RV trailer or rig they can obtain to live this alternative nomadic lifestyle. Vanlifer's economic abilities range from relying on handouts and help, to living on social security, to working while traveling, and those who are financially stable, yet chose this lifestyle for its lure of minimalism and immersion in nature.

While these individuals and the grassroots communities and caravans of like-minded souls are ever-evolving, the rest of society is slow to accept this form of alternative dwelling. Cities and towns struggle with the homeless, and are not sure how to deal with the houseless who live in a vehicle. Granted, in many cases, these rundown, and often non-running RVs or vans that remain permanently parked are no less a civic hassle than dealing with homeless tent cities. And yet, they are part of our society, and society is mostly failing to help them live a life of dignity in a safe and healthy manner.

Unfortunately, many places often view run-down RV dwellers in the same light as $100,000 camper vans spending a quiet night on a back street. While police usually deal with each type differently, local lawmakers often bunch them together into an undesirable group and create laws to prohibit them from within their city or town boundaries.

VANLIFE'S FUTURE?

Still, the vanlife subculture continues to grow significantly with refugees escaping brick-and-mortar houses and lifestyles. In recent years, the COVID-19 pandemic contributed to an explosion of new RV owners looking for a way to travel or escape the stress of dealing with pandemic risks. This expansion put a strain on formal campgrounds, related vanlife resources, and vehicle parts and services, especially for RVs and similar vehicles. The influx brought a lot of newbies into the camping and vanlife world who do not know or follow the long-held courtesies and rules.

RVers and vanlifers can take some of the blame for increased restrictions and blowback from communities because of bad behavior and disregard for the cities and towns they stay in. Those of us who are on good behavior help offset the bad players, but like many things in life, the few spoil things for the many.

Places that used to be available for overnighters like Cabela's or WalMart began prohibiting overnighting. Cabela's even dropped services supporting the RVers. And who can blame them? These retailers have to pay the unexpected cost of trash removal and abandoned items cleanup, store customers hassled by residents of these rolling homes, and parking lots looking like junkyards. Add to that, sadly, an increase in altercations with local law enforcement, and it is understandable how the shift from accommodating the vanlife community to banning them came about.

Despite these declining resources, there is good news.

Depending on your vehicle, there are still many locations to overnight if you are careful, quiet, and most of all, tidy and well behaved! There are still millions of acres of federal land out there to use for short- or long-term stays (though the majority of this land is in the western half of the United States).

MY VANLIFE STORY

I have camped off-and-on throughout my life, but only recently devoted full-time focus to vanlife traveling and immersion in nature. After retiring from corporate life, I sold my house, most of my possessions, and bought a Class B Winnebago Travato. I spent most of a year traveling America and getting used to vanlife and embracing the home on wheels lifestyle. After selling the Travato in the eve of the Covid pandemic, I, as everyone else, had to be content with dreams of someday traveling again after the pandemic was over.

As things progressed and we learned how to be safe, I experimented with building a camper conversion in my Subaru Outback. The freedom of a car versus a larger van or RV is enticing, but I soon learned that although the Outback camper option was fantastic for brief trips or weekends, I yearned to hit the road again in a self-contained rig for longer periods of time.

That brought me to the choice of either buying an empty van and building my conversion, or buying something already converted. I knew the specific features I wanted in this new van: the space to stand up inside; much shorter length than the Travato to allow easy parking anywhere; and as self-contained as possible, so I could extend stays in the wild, relying on whatever resources the van carried or could generate.

Since the pandemic shutdown delayed my travel plans for over a year, I was not interested in waiting for the many months it would take to build out a van. Instead, I purchased a Winnebago Solis Pocket, a new camper van debuted in the summer of 2021. It had features that matched most of my want list, and what it lacked, I could add or modify to get my ideal van.

That van is what I am now roaming America in as I write this. Those experiences, plus travels in the previous two vehicles, influenced the tips, tricks, and suggestions explored throughout this book.

Ready to create your want list and find answers to your questions about modern nomadic vanlife?

Let's go!

CHAPTER 2
WHY CHOOSE VANLIFE?

> Long term travel is not an act of rebellion against society;
> it's an act of common sense within society.

ROLF POTTS

Why would anyone give up the comforts of home, such as a fully equipped kitchen and endless hot-water showers? Or the simplicity of mail and packages delivered to your doorstep? Or a convenient washer and dryer?

In short: *Why choose vanlife?*

There are as many answers as types of people and variety of situations. For some, vanlife can provide a dignified option instead of becoming homeless. For others, it may mean embracing a simpler lifestyle of traveling, pursuing amazing adventures, and reaching new horizons. Whichever is your reason, being informed and knowledgeable about the pros and cons will help you transition to vanlife.

VANLIFE DEFINED

Before we get too far: *What is vanlife?*

My definition is: "an alternative lifestyle using a mobile vehicle to live a nomadic existence while traveling and camping with relative ease and comfort."

A modern nomad is a mobile nomad. Those who live in a vehicle by necessity and do not move it (usually because it does not run), may be better off than in a homeless tent or living under a bridge. I do not include that culture as part of vanlife. Granted, vanlifers frequently stay in one spot for long periods, but they eventually move to a different location.

For this book, the term vanlife covers the lifestyle of living and traveling in a vehicle, whether part-time, full-time, or on extended vacations. Your chosen vehicle could be a car, car with trailer, minivan, pickup (with or without a hard shell or camper insert), cargo van, camper van, RV motorhome or trailer, school bus, or something esoteric, like a used ambulance or converted delivery truck. The variety encountered in vanlife is seemingly endless. I am always impressed by the different ways people adapt vehicles for this lifestyle.

VANLIFE'S PROS & CONS

Pros:

- Inexpensive alternative to a traditional apartment or house

- Dignified lifestyle for those who lose their jobs or house, versus homeless in tents or under bridges, etc.

- Option to travel and explore new areas and cultures

- Healthier, simpler approach to life and possessions

- Freedom of choice in where and when you go, plus the ability to quickly move on if a place makes you uncomfortable

- Mobile internet access for those who need to work on the road

- Comfort in having a bed, bathroom, and kitchen anywhere, whether visiting friends or family, or attending events

- Expense of a hotel room, etc., avoided

- Safer way to travel during a pandemic because you control exposure to people and places

- Access to natural places such as National Parks, or boondocking on wild U.S. Forest land, or Bureau of Land Management (BLM) locations

- Weather event flexibility, i.e., driving away from adverse weather

Cons:

- Loneliness or isolation possible

- Challenging if your vehicle needs repair, you get sick, or encounter uncomfortable situations or people

- Gas, insurance, and initial cost of setting up a vehicle can be expensive, depending on your vehicle type

- Living space limited compared to an apartment or house; requires a different approach to things and a shift in assumptions regarding comfort and material options

- Storage costs can be expensive to hold onto items you wish to keep, but cannot bring with you

- Challenging to receive mail or packages

- Arranging health care appointments and procedures can be complicated, with flexibility necessary on who you see or where you obtain healthcare support on the road

The list of cons should not discourage you, since most have possible solutions, although they may require openness, patience, and a willingness to try new things. Those who adopt vanlife over homelessness may struggle with these cons, but can eventually learn the workarounds.

Regardless of your reasons for transitioning to vanlife, there are a few aspects most successful vanlifers embrace: love of driving and traveling, and enjoying their own company (or the company of their traveling companion, if present). If you do not enjoy these aspects, then vanlife may be more challenging than expected.

IS VANLIFE RIGHT FOR YOU?

Is there an ideal type of person best suited to vanlife?

Probably, but that should not stop anyone from taking advantage of what vanlife can offer. There are many approaches: from minimalist to survivalist, as a rolling workplace or cozy haven, or even glamping and traveling in high style. It is all about what works for you.

Vanlife works well for couples, families, solo travelers of any gender, and even traveling with pets. I know full-time vanlife families who homeschool their children while creating amazing experiences and memories. Vanlife's adaptability via different vehicles and approaches makes it workable for almost anyone.

Ultimately, vanlife may mean a significant change in how one lives. Thus, having awareness of your expectations and reservations will help you adapt. Understanding your thoughts and intentions for living this way should lead you to that *"I am sure"* moment when you finally roll down the road in your home on wheels.

MANIFESTO EXERCISE

To help explore this concept more fully, and test whether it is right for you, consider going through a manifesto exercise. A manifesto is a declaration of intention, opinion, objective, or motive about a topic or issue you are passionate about. The process helps you explore your thoughts and better understand your reasons to adopt vanlife, both apparent and less-obvious.

When doing this exercise, consider what you believe vanlife will give you, why you believe it, and what changes or improvements in your personal behaviors and actions you expect to come from the nomadic living experience.

I developed my vanlife manifesto starting with a mindstorming session. I wrote down whatever came to mind without censoring or editing my thoughts. The following list of keywords and phrases from that effort helped me understand why and how nomadic vanlife appealed to me. Your list could be similar or quite different.

- Accepting change better
- Attention to self
- Bucket list destinations
- Cheaper living costs
- Contemplation
- Danger or situations easily avoided by driving away
- Dealing with whatever happens
- Faith in abilities to react to situations
- Food, eating, and other things under my control
- Freedoms
- Immersion
- Love of driving
- Minimalism
- Nature
- Nimbleness
- Randomness
- Reading opportunity

- Recharging my introvert energies
- Safety from pandemic
- Simplicity
- Solitary, solitude
- Time for writing poetry
- Time to learn to sketch better
- Varied scenery
- And others more obscure

Your manifesto can be finalized bullet lists under topic headings, or in essay form. Whichever approach you choose, your manifesto can help guide your vanlife experience and if needed, help remind you later why you chose this lifestyle.

CHAPTER 3
FROM HOUSELIFE
TO VANLIFE

> I feel like I belong to a different culture now. An older, nomadic one. I feel like I belong to the woods and stars and not at all to the houses.

LUCY LETCHER

At a basic level, houselife and vanlife share similar functions and processes. The differences occur mostly in scale and magnitude of items and processes, plus the radical difference in available space. That limitation in a van does not mean giving up everything you like to do, but it does mean you may need to alter your approach, and in some cases, let go of wants.

For instance, in your house or apartment you may enjoy sprawling on your sectional sofa to read the New York Times newspaper on a lazy Sunday morning. Vanlife does not mean giving that up, but does mean changing how you do it. Instead of a physical paper, read it digitally. Instead of your sectional, sit outside in a comfy camp chair. Or, there may be a nearby coffee shop where you could buy a paper, and perhaps even find a sofa for your sprawling enjoyment, just like at home.

Other things require a shift in material objects, or rethinking how to do things. Your home kitchen is likely stocked with an assortment of kitchen appliances and a myriad of cooking bowls, implements, and eight or more place settings and silverware. You can still be a gourmet cook in vanlife, but you need to adjust to using fewer tools, dishes, and silverware. See "Chapter 6: Happy Tummy, Happy Nomad" for more on kitchen and cooking stuff.

There are many other areas where, with simplifications, eliminations, or substitutions, you can still do a scaled down version of what you did at home. Remember, vanlife's benefits will offset these sacrifices and alterations.

PREPARING FOR VANLIFE

What follows may or may not apply entirely to you, depending on how you start your vanlife, but is worth reading and absorbing even if doing vanlife part-time or in vacation style. These suggestions and guidelines are mostly for full-time travelers (living in the van most or all of the year), or part-timers (frequent, multi-month travels, with short visits back at a home base).

GOING FULL-TIME

Dealing With Property

Those who rent a home can time their vanlife departure for the end of their lease, arrange a sub-lease, or buy out the lease. If you own your home you can either sell it (as I did), or rent it out while traveling. Some need to sell their home to help finance their vehicle, and choose to avoid the hassle of renting their property.

Either way, it is possible to have a gap between getting out of your home and being ready to hit the road. Options exist for short-term furnished rooms, apartments, or homes, if you cannot stay with friends or family.

When I placed my home up for sale, I expected it would take three to four months to sell. It sold within 48 hours and closed within a month. Now what would I do? Vanlife departure was still six months away! Fortunately, I was able to find a furnished apartment until it was time for me to begin vanlife.

Dealing With Stuff

Some decide, through need or want, to radically minimize their possessions and start vanlife with a vehicle as their primary (and often only) home for the foreseeable future. This lifestyle can be rewarding, and, for some, the difference between living more in your control, than the unknowns and challenges of a homeless park or worse. Or, it can be a conscious choice to radically shift from a life of consumerism and being what others expect you to be.

For those who choose full-time, there is a transition period during which hard decisions are necessary, e.g., downsizing material possessions and disposing of, or making arrangements for, current housing.

- *If your shift to vanlife is a **need**,* then choices are somewhat easier, but likely difficult emotionally. Knowing you have to reduce things to only what fits in a vehicle is tough, but necessary to accept.

- *If your shift to vanlife is a **want**,* then you have the luxury of choice and more control on downsizing material things. Often this can mean generating money from the effort to help offset vanlife start-up costs.

Many vanlifers need to hold on to some things not traveling with them, such as family mementos, etc. In conversations with other full-timers, I heard many creative solutions to the challenge of what to do with stuff kept, but not in the van.

When I sold my home and many of my possessions to go full-time vanlife, what remained would easily fit in a 10 × 10 storage unit. Instead, I rented a friend's small, spare room to store my remaining stuff. Others rent storage units, accept offers of unused space at a family or friend's place, or even empty space at a shop or office. I later learned a few of these full-time vanlifers eventually downsized further, with little left to store outside their traveling vehicle. Often when people store possessions and do not see or use them for long periods, they realize those things no longer matter to them.

There is more than one way to downsize; it depends on each person's ability to handle emotionally decisions about what to store, sell, donate, recycle, or trash from possessions amassed over years. It may surprise you how much stuff you have, and how much is never used. Expect downsizing to take much longer than you think to decide what to keep, store, or let go.

The best advice I read about downsizing was to be aware of your emotions as you go through your possessions. If you are lingering over something, or getting upset about letting go of it, put it aside in a "later" box, thus deferring the decision. After you go through the bulk of your possessions and become more comfortable with the sell, donate, recycle, dispose process, you may be emotionally ready to go back and deal with that "later" box.

During this downsizing effort, try to keep in mind why you are doing this: the benefits of your new vanlife, and letting go of stuff and the responsibility for it. Reducing stuff can be an amazing, empowering process.

Legal Addresses

For full-time vanlifers, establishing a new legal residency is necessary if you sold your home or vacated your apartment. Some full-timers choose to use a relative's address as their residency. This approach does have issues, mostly from a lack of personalized proof of your residency, and perhaps a concern about family or friends snooping in your mail.

I recommend taking advantage of the relaxed residency requirements for establishing your legal domicile of record in one of these three states:

- Florida
- South Dakota
- Texas

Note that two other states (Nevada and Washington) offer similar programs, but most full-time vanlifers choose one of the above three states.

Each of these have somewhat different requirements and required documents. To find out which works best for you, see "Chapter 12: Those Pesky Rules & Requirements, Residency" and "Appendix B – Resources & Links." Each of these state's domicile residency requirements meet the needs for a driver's license, vehicle registration and insurance, and voter's registration. Applicants *do need a valid postal address;* fortunately there are fee-based mail forwarding services in these states that can provide this. Although the address is really a postal box, it works for these residency needs. See the "Mail & Packages" section below for more details.

There are a few institutions that do not accept these domicile addresses. Most financial and investment entities require a physical home address. For these, using a friend or family member's address usually works.

Mail & Packages

Although many probably receive emails for much of what we used to get through postal mail, occasionally other important items arrive via postal mail. For the vanlife traveler, this is where a fee-based mail forwarding service will help. Most of these services will scan your mail for online review. After viewing or saving the PDF, you can request they shred that item. They can also forward accumulated mail at your request to an address of your choice when you want to receive the physical mail.

While these forwarding services are a great resource for most postal mail, forwarding charges for magazines and packages are expensive because of weight or size. If you use a mail forwarding service, consider cancelling your magazine subscriptions and converting them to digital subscriptions to view online.

Packages should also not arrive at your mail-forwarding address because of the high forwarding costs. Instead, have these sent to friend's house along your route, use the General Delivery service available at some small post offices (call ahead, as availability of this service varies), or depend on Amazon orders delivered via their Amazon Locker program to a convenient location along your route. Their growing list of locker locations means most places will likely have somewhere to receive your packages. Note some locations restrict the size of the packages they can accept, or lockers can be too full to accept new packages, but Amazon will advise you of those issues during your order process.

Another possible option for mail forwarding and package delivery is at some RV parks or campgrounds, if staying for a week or more. Not all places offer this, so check if it is critical to your decision to stay there.

For extended stays, probably the best option for mail and packages is when you stay at a BLM (Bureau of Land Management) LTVA (long-term visitor area) in the U.S. Most have places that accept mail and packages nearby, along with other services. When I stayed during the winter of 2021-22 for almost four months at an LTVA near Yuma, AZ, I took advantage of the nearby mail services. There I received Amazon packages, goods from other vendors shipped via UPS and FEDEX, and important postal mail.

Getting goods on the road these days is fairly easy, but does require planning to align shipping times with where you intend to travel through or stay.

GOING PART-TIME

Part-time vanlife may not have the radical changes full-time has, but there are specific part-time items to consider. Part-timers usually do not give up their homes, but they could still choose to purchase a smaller house, or even sell their house and rent something smaller. Those decisions depend on your financial situation and willingness to leave your home empty while you are away for months at times. Some part-timers make those adjustments, often to reduce costs while traveling.

Vanlifers call these "home bases," which have the benefits of familiarity and your own furniture and goods, without needing to change residency or local support services in healthcare, legal assistance, etc.

If you are a part-timer with a home base, you may want to consider a house-sitter or at least a good friend, relative, or neighbor to check for issues or damage, pick up mail and packages, etc.

CHAPTER 4
WHICH NOMADIC HOME
IS RIGHT FOR YOU?

> There was nowhere to go but everywhere, so just keep on rolling under the stars.
>
> JACK KEROUAC

This chapter covers common vehicles you might consider for your nomadic home. Whether adapting something you own, getting a vehicle from a relative or friend, or figuring out the best vehicle you should buy, some research and soul searching is necessary to understand which vehicle is right for you.

ESSENTIAL QUESTIONS

- How do you plan to live and travel in the vehicle: Full-time, part-time, keep a home base?

- Do you plan to carry everything you own in the vehicle?

- Do you anticipate moving around a lot, or mostly staying in one place?

- Is there a limit to what you can afford?

- Can you create a repair fund?

- Do you already have a vehicle, or are you looking for the ideal set of wheels?

- Who will be traveling (solo, couple, or more)?

- Are you taking a pet, or pets?

- Do you need lots of space, or can you adapt to something more efficient?

- Are you planning on seasonal travel (follow the sun, basically) or do you need a four-season vehicle?

- Will you travel mostly on paved roads, or often wander down dirt roads?

You will need to know the most likely answers to each of these questions before you choose a vehicle.

VEHICLE CHOICE OVERVIEW

What are the primary types of vehicles to consider for vanlife? Note that there are always unique and unusual vehicles adaptable to vanlife, but for simplicity we will look at six common types. I suspect most who read this book will not be interested in a Class A or C RVs, but include them for comparison. Typical vanlifers usually travel in a Class B, a cargo/camper van, or a passenger vehicle such as a minivan.

The six types discussed:

- **Cargo van (DIY or custom conversion)** – Commercial cargo van converted by an owner, or one purchased from a custom conversion company (not a production RV).

- **Minivan** – Frequent choice of travelers wanted a lot of space but the convenience of passenger car size and better gas mileage.

- **Motorized RV (motorhomes)** – Commonly range from a Class A (biggest), Class C (mid-size), or Class B (sometimes called camper vans, but basically van-size).

- **Passenger car** (station wagon, SUV, hatchback, etc.) – Gives travelers a choice to sleep inside the car, or within ground or roof tents.

- **Pickup truck w/camper shell attached** – Various configurations, from self-contained within the pickup bed, to larger ones with stabilizer legs and extensions.

- **RV trailer** – Range from house-size trailers, to fifth-wheels trailers pulled by a heavier class pickup, to teardrop trailers, which some small cars can tow. Pop-up campers are also a trailer type.

CARGO VAN

Commercial cargo van converted by the owner, or purchased and delivered to a custom conversion business, this vehicle is probably what many new vanlifers choose. Good for storage, options, traveling on paved or unpaved roads, and suitable for most wild camping situations. A used cargo van can be an affordable option that you build out over time into your ideal vanlife vehicle. You can easily start with an empty van and toss in a bed pad, sleeping bag, and some basic camp kitchen setup, and you are on your way. Traveling with this bare-bones setup can be a great approach to learning what might or might not work for you.

Pros:

- Basic box shell is flexible to design a camper van that fits your needs.

- Easier to stealth camp with since it looks like a work or people van, as opposed to a RV.

- Better gas mileage than most motorized RVs.

- Four-wheel drive can be an option, depending on make and model.

- Ground clearance typically better than a motorized RV.

- Wide range of equipment, materials, and solutions available, since cargo van conversion is a big business in the U.S.

- Can double as a daily driver compared to motorized RVs (smaller Class Bs can potentially be daily drivers, too).

- Wide variety of YouTube videos (tens of thousands, probably) you can watch to learn about cargo van conversions.

- More affordable to convert yourself if you are good with tools and mechanically inclined.

Cons:

- Unless you find one with an extended roof, you cannot stand up inside.

- DIY (do it yourself) conversions can be expensive.

- Even if you are a decent DIYer, you probably should out-source electronics work and anything that involves cutting into the van's exterior skin, e.g., roof vents, windows, anything tying into the chassis electrical, batteries or alternator. It is easy to improperly seal windows, fans, and other equipment cut into the van's metal floor, roof, and sides that could lead to an undetected water leak and cause rust and other water-based damage.

- Outsourced tasks can be expensive and typically have long delays before those providers can do the work.

- If you are buying used, rust problems are common with cargo vans. Be sure to inspect a used van thoroughly, including high-rust-probability areas under driver- and passenger-side mats and floor coverings, rocker panels, wheel fender panels, and frame, including connecting bolts and plates. Best to have an experienced, used-vehicle inspector look for rust damage. Some purchasers who wish to avoid rust issues do not buy a used van driven in a state with wet winters because of increased rust risk. Instead, they search in the south or southwest for vans that have only been driven in those non-winter areas.

- If buying new, the cost of van plus custom conversion may be close to the cost of a ready-made camper van from someone like Winnebago. As of this writing, wait lists for the better-known conversion companies for van conversions commonly run out several years .

MINIVAN

YouTube has a lot of videos showcasing some amazing DIY conversions people did to their minivans to create a viable, more comfortable, high-mpg vanlife vehicle.

Pros and cons are similar to the cargo van above. The same concern with rust occurs in used minivans, and is often unseen by casual inspection. If undetected, rust can later cause serious expense and hassle.

MOTORIZED RVS

Which of these RVs—Class A, B, C, or Camper Van—works for you depends on your intended style of travel, whether you stay in one place for long, and your budget.

CLASS A

- *Length:* ~26 to 45+ feet
- *Weight:* ~6.5 to 15 tons
- *Fuel:* Diesel typically, but smaller Class As run on gasoline
- *Description:* Largest RVs on the road. Interiors are similar to a home, with a designated living area, bedrooms, bathrooms, dining room, and kitchens. Class As have generous storage, typically include washer/dryers, big beds, and are more luxurious than other RV classes. Can pull a vehicle (called a "toad," meaning towed car) so owners can go places, such as running errands, without moving their motorhome. Some Class As, especially shorter ones, have slide-out sections for extending interior space, usually for sleeping, eating, lounging, cooking, etc.
- *Gas mileage:* If you can afford one of these, you likely do not care they get single-digit mpg, and filling the tank costs $$$.
- *Best use:* People who want to travel in the same luxury as they live in at home, with all the obvious comforts and toys. Not ideal for camping in many places because of size, so best for established campgrounds set up to host these big rigs.
- *Exceptions:* Adults traveling in groups or with children will sometimes buy used Class As as more affordable rigs to live and work in while traveling. The limitations noted above apply, even though these RVers are typically not looking for the luxury of home and simply need (or want) more space and amenities for their version of road life. Generally when not used, owners store their Class As at RV storage lots.
- *Typical on-board resources:* Bathrooms with tubs or showers; kitchens with large sinks; ample counter space and cabinet storage; stoves and ovens; microwaves; full-size refrigerators

with freezers; washer/dryers; satellite/Wi-Fi connections and large TVs; large tanks for black and grey waste; large fresh-water tanks; large propane tanks; multiple rooftop fans; multiple air-conditioning units; propane heat. Class As have larger on-board generators, and use 50 amp shore power at campgrounds. Newer Class As usually have solar energy systems.

- *New prices* (*rough estimates; market prices vary*) – $200K to $1 million+
- *Used prices* (*rough estimates; market prices vary*) – $75K to $200k+ (not including repairs to make everything operational)

CLASS C

- *Length:* ~24 to 30+ feet
- *Weight:* ~5 to 6.5+ tons
- *Fuel:* Many are diesel, but some run on gasoline
- *Description:* Scaled-down versions of Class As with some similar features and amenities. Can pull a vehicle (called a "toad," meaning towed car) so owners can go places, such as running errands, without moving their motorhome. Most Class Cs are heavier duty chassis with dual rear wheels because of weight and structural needs. Most Class Cs have an extended area above the driver/passenger cab area, which usually contains sleeping lofts for children or small adults.
- *Gas mileage:* Better than Class As, but typically 10-14 mpg. (Diesels get better.)
- *Best use:* People who want to stay in established campgrounds with inside vehicle space similar to a small apartment (as opposed to Class As, which are more like a house). More luxury and amenities than Class Bs, but typically with similar finishes and equipment. Some Class Cs come with slide-out sections, which extend interior spaces for sleeping, eating, lounging, cooking, etc. Vehicle choice for many solo full-timers who want extra room and are content with mostly using established campgrounds. Class Cs have reasonable mobility

for going into most Federal wilderness lands, but can be difficult to park in cities or maneuver in places designed for cars.

- *Exceptions:* Some newer Class Cs work well for active, sports-minded owners, with gear garages; expanded resource capabilities for electrical, water, etc; more solar capabilities; and additional racks for mounting sports gear. Generally when not used, owners store their Class Cs at RV storage lots. Note that many Homeowners Associations (HOA) may prohibit parking Class Cs (or most RVs) in driveways or on the street for more than a day or two.
- *Typical on-board resources:* Bathrooms with showers, kitchens with propane cooktops, TVs with antennas, black and grey waste tanks, fresh-water tanks, rooftop ventilation, air conditioning, propane heat. Newer models usually have some solar energy capabilities and onboard generators. Class Cs use 30 amp shore power at campgrounds.
- *New prices* (rough estimates; market prices vary) – $185K to $300K+
- *Used prices* (rough estimates; market prices vary) – $75K to $150K+ (not including repairs to make everything operational)

CLASS B

- *Length:* ~17 to 24 feet
- *Weight:* ~2 to 4.5 tons
- *Fuel:* Most have gasoline engines, but those with a Mercedes chassis have diesel engines.
- *Description:* Smallest of the motorized RV classes, with major benefits of better vehicle mobility, capabilities for staying off the grid, better mpg, and a four-wheel-drive option on Mercedes chassis. Class B's compact size encourages a more minimal lifestyle, while still providing for the basic needs of beds, seating, kitchen, bathrooms and sometimes shower. Class Bs are easier to park and navigate in both cities and camping areas. Although Class Bs are smaller than Class Cs, they are

still good for work and travel. Many drivers choose Class Bs for their easier driving and maneuvering, better affordability, and better access to wilderness areas. Thus, these owners are usually more involved in outdoor activities. Not recommended for towing any kind of car, but they can carry bikes on the back doors, or motorbikes via tow hitch carries or small trailer. These options provide Class B owners with some mobility without moving their rig. Some Class Bs have on-board generators.

- *Gas mileage:* 14-18 mpg, typically. (More when highway driving at 60 mph or less, and better mpg on Class Bs with diesel engines.)
- *Best use:* People who value mobility and a minimized, efficient living space. Class Bs typically have extended roofs, allowing owners to stand up inside.
- *Exceptions:* Some Class B designs, such as the Winnebago Revel, support active sports owners with features such as gear garages, and expanded resource capabilities for solar, and four-wheel drive. Note that many Homeowners Associations (HOA) may prohibit parking Class Bs (or RVs in general) in driveways or on the street for more than a day or two.
- *New prices* (rough estimates; market prices vary) – $110K to $200K+
- *Used prices* (rough estimates; market prices vary) – $60K to $150K+ (not including repairs to make everything operational)

PASSENGER CAR

These vehicles (sedan, station wagon, SUV, hatchback, etc.) are viable solutions for those who chose vanlife out of need, and offer a good option to avoid homeless tents or shelters. YouTube has lots of videos from those living full-time in their vehicles after they lost their jobs, residences, or both.

Some drivers create a sleeping space inside their car, while others take a tent to provide a sleeping area, leaving more space inside the vehicle for storage.

These vehicles can be a good way to start vanlife and see if it is right for you, even if you choose vanlife out of want and not need. Starting with a car you own while learning to adapt to life in a vehicle can be a valuable experience before you trade up to something larger.

When living in this option, the two biggest concerns are bathroom needs and weather-related challenges. Many simply take a five-gallon bucket, a make-do toilet seat, and plastic bags to cover their bathroom waste needs. This approach may require creating some type of privacy screening outside, rigged up from tarps, windscreens, or a pop-up cabana. I travel with a pop-up cabana which I set up at camps where I plan to stay five days or longer I use the cabana as a shower, toilet room, or outside dressing area.

Weather can present several problems for passenger car occupants, from being stuck inside a vehicle with little ability to move around, to sleeping outside when the weather is cold or inclement. Many solutions exist to stay warm inside a tent in cold or wet weather, and a simple YouTube search will show how others resolve these challenges.

RV TRAILERS

My experience is only with car camping or motorized RVs. A trailer solution might work for you, so I researched and listed some basic information about trailers below.

When considering any of the trailer types below, be sure to read the trailer cons section for guidance on safely matching a vehicle's towing capability to the trailer towing weight.

Remember that actual towing weight is the combination of the empty trailer weight provided by the manufacturer plus the weight of whatever is stored in the trailer, include liquids such as fresh water.

- *Full-size, full-feature hitch, or fifth-wheel trailer* – These are the Class As of the towable world, which mimic a full-size home, but mobile. If you have a large family, or just want a lot of space and amenities that replicate what you have at home, these could work for you. Requires a vehicle with much greater towing capacity.

- *Pickup camper shell* – A subset of trailers designed to fit in the bed of a full-size pickup, although some models fit smaller pickups. Similar in amenities to smaller trailers, they can be viable if you already own the pickup capable of carrying these.

- *Pop-up trailer* – Small, towable trailer pulled by some cars, SUVs, and pickups. Mainly provides a sleeping area, but some have kitchens. They are soft-sided, so not appropriate for camping in areas with bears.

- *Small, hard-sided, full-feature trailer* – Available trailers such as the Casita or Scamp provide a bed, kitchen, bath, etc., in a compact size. I have met many full-timers in these small trailers, so they are an option if that is your travel style. Good choice if you want a trailer but are uncomfortable towing a large trailer. Typically requires a vehicle with greater towing capacity.

- *Teardrop trailer* – Small, hard-sided mini-trailer pulled by some cars, SUVs, and pickups. Suitable for sleeping, and some have a full kitchen via the outside rear hatch.

Trailer pros & cons:

Pros:

- Provides you with a separate vehicle to explore, or run errands into town while your trailer remains set up at the campsite.

- Is more affordable than motorized RVs, assuming you already own a vehicle capable of towing your desired trailer.

- Provides more space for the money compared to other options.

Cons:

- Towing! Some people are good at towing trailers, but I am not one of them. Difficult to back into campsites without practice. Can be dangerous to drive, especially in high winds, at high speed, or when the trailer has unbalanced contents.

- A safe rule of thumb is to tow a trailer weighing at most 60% of a vehicle's towing capacity (trailer plus contents). If you tow in high winds, pull a trailer up steep or winding roads, or execute an emergency maneuver, that trailer's weight will substantially increase (called stress weight). This could be beyond your car or hitch's towing capabilities, which might cause you to lose control of your trailer, have an accident, and likely seriously damage your car's transmission, suspension, and frame. *As an example*, if your car's tow rating is 3,000 lbs. then you should ideally limit towing trailers that weigh no more than 1,800 lbs.

- Unless your home has ample land, or you live where there are no restrictions, you may have to pay to store your trailer when not in use. Note this could also occur if you live somewhere with deed or HOA restrictions against parking a motorized RV at your house.

SUMMARY

While your choice of vehicle is important, it is not one you must commit to forever. You can change vehicles as your vanlife experience evolves. For some, starting with what you already have makes sense because of the cost of getting started. For others, creating their vision of an ideal vehicle may be a better option. It is not usually a good idea to build what you think is your ideal setup until you have vanlife experience in some form or another. What you think will work is often not the reality once you are living vanlife. This approach is common among beginning vanlifers, and I have yet to meet one who did not remark on the mistakes in layout or equipment in their vehicles after they were on the road for a few months or more.

If you cannot afford to start with something already built out, like a camper van or Class B RV, an empty cargo van is perhaps an ideal vehicle to start vanlife. Such a vehicle is essentially a blank canvas that you can slowly work on as you travel, trying different approaches and solutions, eventually discovering what works best for you. Putting a bed, some storage, a camp kitchen, a camp chair, etc. into your new empty van is cost-effective and quick to get you on the road that much sooner.

One Canadian YouTuber I follow (Vancity Vanlife) started this way and still highly recommends this beginning approach for everyone. He began over four years ago with cheap, disposable plastic drawers, cabinets, bins, a mattress on the floor, a bucket for pooping, and a basic camping stove for cooking. Since then, as he learned what worked for him as he traveled, his van slowly became an example of what is possible.

Some people delay getting into vanlife, consumed with figuring out the best layout, equipment, and gear, thus deny the learning experience of starting with a bare-bones rig. Best to get going now and experience vanlife from the bottom up, rather than wait, guess what you need, and waste money. It is certainly useful to see what others are doing, but file those ideas for later when you have experienced vanlife yourself and understand what works for you.

CHAPTER 5
STAYING IN TOUCH
ON THE ROAD

> Travel far enough, you meet yourself.
>
> DAVID MITCHELL

You have selected your vehicle and begun setting it up for vanlife. Now, consider how you need to prepare for those activities, functions, and situations you previously took for granted while you were living in a house or apartment. At the top of the list may be how you will stay in touch with family, employers, and the rest of the outside world. The following will cover some of what you need to consider regarding connectivity while traveling.

CONNECTIVITY

Equipment

Connectivity equipment I currently travel with:

- *Apple MacBook*

- *Apple iPad Pro* with *Apple Pencil*

- *HP Laserjet M15W printer (replaced by newer model M110W)* – Smallest laser printer available; runs off 110-volt so use it via my inverter or when on shore power

- *Netgear Nighthawk Wi-Fi router* – AT&T, but set up with a phone plan instead of a data plan, thus giving me unlimited data versus limited data on a data-only plan

- *Samsung 27" TV* – For streaming video and as an extended monitor for the MacBook (another 110-volt device run off the inverter or shore power)

- *Two iPhones (AT&T primary, Verizon backup)* – Both are smartphones because there are so many great travel apps available now; see "Appendix B – Resources & Links" for app recommendations

- *WeBoost OTR (over the road) antenna* – Mounted on roof with a spring and hinged base to lay down the antenna for low-clearance situations

- *WeBoost Sleek cellular booster* – iPhone cradle; also works with Netgear router

Other equipment to consider, based on your present or future needs:

- *Satellite receiver* – Usually seen more on Class As, but possible to store and set up on the ground in a campsite for any rig.

- *Tesla Starlink* – Satellite-based solution for phone and internet. Soon to be more common on mobile vehicles.

- *Two-way radios* – Useful if traveling with other vehicles to more easily communicate without relying on cell phones.

- *Wi-Fi booster* – Alternative to traveling with a Wi-Fi hotspot router, these increase Wi-Fi strength and connection options while camped or parked overnight at Walmart, etc. If using a Wi-Fi booster, highly recommend subscribing to a good VPN service and always use it when connecting to public Wi-Fi channels for a more secure connection.

Internet

Cellular connectivity improves each year, and new options appear for connecting to the internet while traveling. I have been in many areas, however, where there still is no cellular signal, or it is too weak for adequate internet access. You can use a cellular booster to improve a weak signal, but a **booster will not help if there is no signal available.**

To improve my chances of finding a signal, I installed a high-end antenna that extends a few feet above my van's roof, which helps in some locations. A MIMO antenna is another option I use that sometimes helps the signal more than the rooftop antenna. This type of antenna requires a cellular router with external antenna ports.

A good cellular hotspot router allows your devices to connect to a Wi-Fi network within and around a vehicle. Depending on your phone or equipment data plans, this type of router can be more economical and provide a better Wi-Fi signal than a cell phone used as a hotspot.

Some campgrounds (most often, organized and fee-based parks) offer public Wi-Fi access, which works well, but is not secure and thus not recommended for accessing any site or service where you use a password. If the park has a lot of campsites occupied, other campers may use the same Wi-Fi, slowing down data speeds. Traveling with your own Wi-Fi router on a cellular plan with a good amount of data means you can avoid those security and streaming issues.

If you prefer to use a public Wi-Fi where you stay, consider installing an amplified Wi-Fi booster, and *always go through a private VPN for a more secure connection.*

Phone

Coverage across the U.S. varies by carrier, with some carriers better in one location versus others. You may travel with two or more networks to give you more options to connect, depending how important constant connectivity is to your needs. See "Appendix B – Resources & Links" for an app to show cellular coverage where you are and another app that locates network cell tower locations (to check your line-of-sight to your network's towers).

PERSONAL CONTACT

Being Social

Before COVID-19 arrived, during my year of post-retirement travel I visited with friends and openly socialized while traveling. I forged some great new friendships with other vanlifers during that time. Now my vanlife is significantly more isolated by design, and socializing with strangers that could become new friends is rare.

While some vanlifers still meet up and congregate with others on the road, I choose to continue mostly isolated travel, since as of this writing, the U.S. COVID-19 contagion and risk remains high. Despite being vaccinated and boosted, my approach is still a cautious one. How you choose to behave is, of course, up to you, but I would suggest extra diligence while on the road since getting sick from COVID-19 while living in a vehicle would be challenging.

I do, however, stay in touch with friends and family through social media and cellular phone while I travel, provided I stay at places with good internet connectivity.

Friendship

Modern life means instant connectivity with anyone anywhere in the world. Whether via a phone call, Face Time or Skype video calls, or chats/messages, vanlife does not mean isolation from friends and family. With the proper setup, you can connect via phone or internet-based options in most of the areas you will travel.

One benefit of this lifestyle is the community comprised of people, like yourself, who have chosen this way to live and travel. You may meet vanlifers on the road and in campgrounds who become new, long-term friends. I have lost count of how many strangers became friends after a day of visiting. Vanlifers are usually generous, and many times these quick friendships include offers to stay in their driveways, repair parts, or advice on where to stay or where to avoid. The most pleasant surprise for me since embracing vanlife has been discovering this community and the difference it makes while traveling, camping, and taking care of your vehicle.

Networks

Facebook Groups focused on vanlife, lifestyle travelers, or the specific vehicle rig you have, are another strong networking option. The Face-book Group for my van, the Solis Pocket, is my go-to source for technical help, maintenance questions, troubleshooting, and socializing with others who own and love the same camper van. Such networks provide some comfort and assurance when a problem arises, as opposed to relying on RV repair dealerships.

Unfortunately, over the past several years, the difficulty of getting a timely repair appointment with many RV dealers increased with long wait times common. This situation opened the door for a booming mobile RV repair market, but while these mobile businesses may be more responsive, they may not be a solution for you if your repair is still under warranty, although under special situations you may be reimbursed.

There are fewer good, responsive RV dealers out there than you might think. If you own a RV and need warranty repair, the dealer you bought it from is your best option for reasonably quick service. See "Chapter 9: Vehicle Stuff – Challenges & Solutions, Maintenance" for more information.

WORKING ON THE ROAD

Not all who wander are… retired!

Some vanlifers need to continue working as they travel. With some planning and positional awareness (for optimum internet connection), many work successfully on the road, whether supporting their current full-time job, working as freelancers, or running their own business while traveling. I know of one full-time vanlifer who continued his eBay business when he shifted from houselife to vanlife. Some clever rearranging in the van allowed him to store enough stock to sell and ship while traveling.

Pre-pandemic, other vanlifers I met did arts and crafts shows around the country. They not only carried their goods to each show, but also set up their RV so they could create their goods while living full-time on the road. I met one artist in a Class C RV who pulled a trailer carrying panels he used to display his oil paintings at art fairs around the country. He dedicated his front passenger seat to be his painting studio. At the RV park where I met him, I would often see him sitting with his easel arranged in front of him, looking out the front wind-shield and painting the scene in his view.

Most of the travelers I have met, though, were tech workers, writers, and similar professionals who used computers and required fast, reliable internet connections.

If working while traveling is a need but you think it is too challenging, search YouTube for stories of vanlifers successfully working on the road, many as full-timers. One obstacle may be your employer, who will not allow you to work remotely. Perhaps another employer in the same industry would embrace this option, especially because working from home worked so well during the COVID-19 pandemic. Remember that vanlife usually means less income needed, which may open up more opportunities to find remote work that meets your needs.

CHAPTER 6
HAPPY TUMMY, HAPPY NOMAD

> Cooking and eating food outdoors makes it taste infinitely better than the same meal prepared and consumed indoors.

FENNEL HUDSON

A good meal can be the highlight of a day. The pleasures of picking out just the right ingredients, preparing them, then enjoying the result with friends or alone, is comfort for the soul.

One difference in vanlife over homelife is that food has a slightly bigger importance. If you are a solo traveler, a good meal becomes a self-reward that can help soothe any lingering loneliness. For those who see eating as merely fueling their bodies, there is still the incentive of being creative with ingredients while traveling. A high point of many of my weeks on the road is when I get to restock the van with fresh foods and serendipitous goodies.

While cooking for one is not as much fun as cooking for more, it is still an opportunity for present-mindedness and reflection on the day, not to mention a treat to your taste buds, and that satisfying feeling after eating a good meal.

SCALING DOWN TO VANLIFE

With a basic kitchen and a cooler or refrigerator, you can cook your own meals. This has multiple benefits, especially if you have allergies or special dietary needs.

Unless you are in a generously sized Class A or C RV, shifting your thinking is necessary to stock a vanlife kitchen with just the right amount of dishes, cooking pots, utensils, and appliances to cook how you like to eat. The section "Cooking & Kitchen Tools" below goes into more detail.

Most vanlife vehicles have limited space for food. Your vanlife refrigerator or cooler will probably only hold a fraction of what your expansive freezer and refrigerator could at home. It may take more effort and forethought to stock your vehicle with the right variety and quantity of food, as well as changing the quantities you prepare, e.g., make no more than enough for the one meal, plus one leftover serving.

FOOD SHOPPING & STORAGE

New vanlifers need to relearn how to food shop and adapt to the storage limitations for pantry and refrigerator/freezer. Used to stocking up at CostCo? Sorry, such bulk stores are not good places to shop in vanlife. Habitually buy in quantity to save? Not going to be helpful, either. Vanlife food is about finding the right balance between what you need or want, what you have room to carry, and how often you shop. The answer to the last part is "more often than before."

Part of the challenge is avoiding food spoilage. Buying just enough perishable food to last without going bad is a learned skill.

In your home or apartment, stocking up on food that did not require refrigeration or freezing helped keep more options on hand. Unless you drive a Class A RV, those options are not present during vanlife. Becoming good at estimating the right amount of food to buy and travel with starts by considering meals you plan to make.

Guidelines and suggestions on food shopping and storage:

- Buy smaller amounts of goods requiring consumption soon, e.g., most produce, deli meats, raw meats/fish.

- Optimize freezer choices based on importance to you. Do you want ice available? Then that is less room for frozen foods. Limit frozen items to one of each (one pound of ground beef, etc.), and perhaps repackage them to fit in the freezer better. Ice cream may not fit in some freezers unless repackaged. For leftovers, use refrigeration instead of freezing, which means eating leftovers within the next two meals.

- Choose items with less packaging, and become a master in the art of repacking before storing, whether in the refrigerator, freezer, or pantry. Ziploc® bags are great for this. Remember to spend time in the grocery store parking lot repackaging, and take advantage of their trash receptacles to toss, or hopefully recycle, the old packaging.

- Limit spices to only those used frequently. Vanlife is easier if you can reduce the spices you carry to those you use frequently. Avoid carrying spare spices: when you run out, buy a replacement on the road.

- Buy dry goods (oatmeal, grains, beans, lentils, rice, nuts, seeds, etc.) in small quantities and accept buying them more frequently

Guidelines and suggestions on foods requiring freezing or refrigeration:

- Buy only essential items requiring freezing or refrigeration in two-portion serving sizes or less, unless you have ample room.

- Reduce freezer or refrigerator items to their smallest mass (repackage to Ziploc® bags), and trim produce to only what is edible. Remember to do this in the grocery store parking lot and use their trash receptacles for the waste.

- Store non-refrigerated produce (e.g., citrus, apples, tomatoes) in a produce hammock or basket. You still need to monitor these before they go bad, but they will last reasonably well in the hammock and not take up valuable refrigerator space.

- Avoid liquids such as milk or juices, unless UHT-labeled (ultra-high temperature processing which makes them safe to store without refrigeration before opening), or in small containers, because of bulk that takes up disproportional storage space.

- Chill only a few beverage cans or one bottle of wine/beverage at a time in the refrigerator. Store extras in your general storage area in your vehicle, saving room in the pantry for other types of dry food.

- Plan to use jarred foods (nut butters, mayo, salsa, etc.) quickly, or limit how many of these are simultaneously open and stored in the refrigerator.

- Limit choices to just one type of certain items, e.g., one hummus, one nut butter, one sandwich spread, one salad dressing.

- Find double uses for items where possible. I buy Ezekiel English Muffins that work as breakfast muffins or sandwich breads. I sometime use tortillas or Romaine lettuce instead of sandwich bread to save space. Breads are difficult to manage in a vehicle since they can mold quickly. To counter this, I always store my muffins and tortillas in the refrigerator, which limits how much of those I buy.

COOKING & KITCHEN TOOLS

How you cook, and what you eat on and with, also needs a few efficiency and economy tweaks. The simple rule is: Less is better, multipurpose utensils ideal, and developing new and minimal cooking methods and habits helpful.

Ideas and guidelines:

- Adopt the one thing approach, if solo traveling: One dish, one bowl, one coffee mug, etc. If you plan to feed company occasionally, then splurge and go with two of each of those.

- Carry two forks, knives, spoons and two cutting knives, whether solo or with company, since these get dirty more often and you may need multiples when preparing meals. Carry a minimum of cooking utensils (spatula, big spoon, etc.)

- Limit pots and pans to one small skillet, one large skillet, one small pot, if solo. Add a larger pot if two or more people are traveling. For cleaning ease and to avoid wasting water, use non-stick pans with a healthy, non-toxic coating.

- Know that small pans work best. In most cases, your cooking source will be a camp stove or propane cooktop. The burners for these are smaller than your home cooktops, thus smaller pans work better. Note that items with long cooking times, such as rice or stews consume a lot of your propane resource. Consider options requiring shorter times, e.g., precooked rice, canned soup, etc.

- Take advantage of cooking over a campfire if available, particularly for odorous foods like fish or seafood. I carry a stainless steel grill to put over a campfire or camp-provided grills.

- Consider cooking some foods while you drive. One energy-efficient alternative is the Hot Logic Mini or Max, a 12v slow-cook device to cook meats, fish, and other foods while driving. A Hot Logic cooks most foods in two hours and does not smell up the vehicle.

- Take small appliances along only if your vehicle can use shore power, has lithium batteries, or you invest in a large portable solar generator (e.g., Jackery) with enough power to run an appliance. Without such appliances you can still mix, blend, toast, or boil water in other ways, but it takes more time. I installed lithium batteries and an inverter in my van and travel with these small appliances: small rice cooker, toaster, blender stick, and electric tea kettle. Before that upgrade, I made toast in a frying pan, steamed rice in a pot, and boiled water for tea and coffee on my propane stove.

COFFEE OR TEA?

Enjoying a great cup of coffee or a nice cup of tea made in my van is a highlight of most of my vanlife days. I love getting up early and greeting the sunrise while sipping a fresh cup of coffee that I did not have to drive, or even get out of my pajamas to get. Making coffee or tea in vanlife is one process that can be quite different, depending if you are brewing for one person or several.

Some tips and the processes I use:

Coffee:

- **Pour over** is a favorite option for many vanlifers. This process involves using a pour over funnel with a #2 filter, and hot water made on a propane stove, or an electric water kettle, if equipped. This method is a nice, slow practice that helps me ease into the day. I also chose this method to save water, a critical vanlife resource to monitor. Using the hand pour method requires very little water to clean, and tossing the filter with grounds eliminates rinsing out mesh filters, French presses, etc., which can require a lot of water.

- Some travelers prefer **K cup machines**, which work well, but only if on shore power or your vehicle has lithium batteries or generator.

- If you need to make coffee for two or more, pour over still works, but it takes time. Coffee drinkers who want their morning java quickly probably want a **large French press or other non-electric method** to make several cups at the same time.

- **Storing coffee** is also different in vanlife. Since coffee is best when freshly ground, ideally carry only one bag of grounds and replenish on the next food run. Alternately, adopt my method: Grind two types of coffee, store some of the grounds in small, stainless steel coffee containers, and the excess in the back of the refrigerator. I used to only carry beans and use a single-use hand grinder, but that method repeated every day over a long period was tiring. I also do not have patience to wait that long for the first cup most mornings!

- If you use K-cups, then the only limit on what you can take is your storage space. I traveled with a K-cup machine in my Travato during 2019 and enjoyed using it when I was in a campground or other places providing shore power. Now, I prefer the peaceful process and increased control using the hand pour method.

Tea:

- More process- and space-efficient than coffee, making hot tea usually only requires boiling water and tea bags (or small filter bags into which you put loose tea). Whether you are solo or traveling with two or more, the setup and brew time for one or several cups is the same. How you boil the water varies depending on your vehicle's energy options, as mentioned in the Coffee section.

CLEANING UP & WASTE

In my pre-van days of tent camping, I learned the art of cleaning dirty dishes quickly while conserving water. I produced a video of how to do this on an early Subaru Outback camping experiment that you can watch here. This method continues to be my daily method for washing dirty dishes, except those that are oily, or had raw egg or meat. For those instances, I use a grease-cutting dishwasher soap instead of vinegar.

The cold water/vinegar combo has a long history, and most campers consider it safe. I have used this method for more years than I can remember and never got sick from poorly cleaned dishes. Note it is an ideal method for solo travelers and those traveling in vehicles with limited counter space and water. Those who travel in larger vehicles, such as Class C or A RVs, likely clean their dishes as they did at home: soap and hot water.

I clean non-egg/oils/raw meat dishes using three tools: fresh water spray bottle, vinegar water (50-50) spray bottle, and paper towels.

*Steps for **soapless** cleaning:*

1. Wipe the item with a paper towel to remove food residue.
2. Spray with water, wipe with a paper towel.
3. Spray with vinegar, wait about a minute, wipe and dry with a paper towel.

*Steps for **soap** cleaning (dirty dishes with egg/oils/raw meat):*

1. Wipe the dish/bowl/cup/pot with a paper towel to remove food residue.
2. Put a few drops of Dawn or other grease-cutting dish soap into a clean bowl, then add some water and stir to make suds.
3. Dip a sponge into that bowl and clean the dirty dish.
4. Rinse quickly with water, and use the spray water bottle to reduce water waste.
5. Set aside on a drying mat or in a rack to air dry.

Ultimately, it helps to reduce cleanup by using as few dishes as possible to prepare or eat on. That is another good habit to shift between homelife and vanlife.

EATING OUT

Many vanlifers choose to eat out often, and thus reduce cooking in their vehicles. This approach means less shopping, but probably means buying more treats and snacks to travel with. Eating out in vanlife may not be a good idea if you have severe dietary restrictions or during events such as a pandemic.

Vanlife vehicles can easily be a great place to cook and eat without going to restaurants. During my last travels, over the course of five months I ate out maybe a dozen times, with all but two take-outs. I am living and traveling proof you can eat healthy and with variety out of your vehicle nearly every day you travel.

WHAT ABOUT PIZZA DELIVERY?

Maybe! If an organized campground or RV park is close to a town with pizza delivery, it is possible to treat yourself with delivery pizza. It depends whether the pizza place can get into your campground/park, and the delivery people will likely know. Worth a shot, now and then! I actually love cold leftover pizza in the morning. Yeah, I know… weird, but not uncommon!

CHAPTER 7
PERSONAL STUFF – CHALLENGES & SOLUTIONS

> To my mind, the greatest reward and luxury of travel is to be able to experience everyday things as if for the first time, to be in a position in which almost nothing is so familiar it is taken for granted.

BILL BRYSON

Many people who start vanlife do not realize how much there is to deal with on a personal level. Some think vanlife will be a simpler, more minimalistic experience. And it is, to some degree. There are, however, some differences in dealing with personal things in vanlife.

DOCUMENTS & RESOURCES

Carry a hidden stash box somewhere in your vehicle. Within this box could be your passport, insurance cards, emergency cash ($500-1,000 if possible), vital legal papers, spare credit card, extra blank checks, and if traveling with a pet, their inoculation records. What about a spare key/key fob? Absolutely take one of those, but you may prefer to find a good hiding place outside your locked vehicle and not in the stash box.

EXERCISE

Continuing a healthy exercise practice on the road is easy, although it may require a different daily approach. The health and well-being that exercise enables is important when traveling, perhaps more so if you spend a lot of time driving. Vanlifers should assess the exercises they do at home and adapt them for life on the road.

Some common exercise practices and tips for vanlife:

- **Biking** – Many vanlifers travel with pedal bikes (or e-bikes) for their exercise choice. Typically, bikes mount on a trailer hitch rack, a rear-door-mounted rack, or are stored inside the vehicle if there is room. A good lock (or double locks) is necessary if you carry your bikes outside the vehicle.

- **Kayaks** – You will see many vans traveling with kayaks on roof racks so those vanlifers can continue their love of this sport and the exercise benefits it provides.

- **Resistance training** – This exercise is more challenging in vanlife, especially if you are used to a local fitness place and their exercise machines. Two options that work in vanlife are taking a few 2-5 lb. barbells and a pack of resistance bands. With these, you can design a decent resistance program and not lose the good work built up at a fitness center. Check out YouTube for examples of daily routines that work for nomads. Alternatively, if you join a fitness franchise to access their showers while traveling, stay a while longer and use their exercise machines. Combining occasional fitness center visits between resistance band/barbell routines, yoga, and walking is a great way to stay in shape during your vanlife travels.

- **Walking** – A daily walk is not only good cardio exercise, it also helps to relieve stress and get you outside! Walking around a campground is one option, but it can be far better to take advantage of nearby trails for long walks. Even if stealth-camped in a city, walks are easy to include in one's daily exercise routine.

- **Yoga** – A yoga mat takes up little room and is easy to unroll in the morning for campsite yoga. Yoga is a fantastic way to maintain flexibility and stay limber, especially if a lot of your vanlife is sitting and driving. Sage advice from my doctor: "Motion is lotion," and "Flexibility is the fountain of youth."

GETTING SICK

Vanlifers cannot predict when or if they get sick any more than they could at home, but there are things they can do to prepare for this uncomfortable situation. Beyond the recommendations mentioned in the "Healthcare" section below, be sure to maintain a clean water supply, dump waste regularly, and keep food supplies stocked. Do not risk food contamination by eating food that is about to go bad.

Proactive steps you can take to help minimize the impact of sickness include eating healthy, exercising frequently, getting good sleep, and maintaining your program of prescriptions and supplements. Another obvious proactive measure is to make most, if not all, of your own vehicle- or campsite-made meals from real food, i.e., mostly fresh or dry goods, while avoiding processed foods.

Vanlife can easily feel like a vacation where you overeat, drink too much, eat outside your diet, stay up late, etc. This is easy to do, but it can compromise your health and resistance to sickness. Live your vanlife as you would if you were at home, and do the proactive things that keep you healthy and well.

Making your own meals can also reduce the risk of food-borne bacteria and reactions. However, it is still possible to contract bacteria from grocery store food. Along with the other proactive steps, be sure to rinse produce when you bring it into your vehicle. Learning how much produce you can consume before it goes bad is a good skill to develop.

If you get sick to the point you need help, most cities or towns have either hospital emergency rooms, or at least an emergency clinic. In small towns, it is often possible to see a physician on short notice and avoid the higher-fee emergency rooms and clinics. On my vanlife travels, I have needed a doctor twice, a dentist once, and an optometrist once. Fortunately, these were accessible because I was in a good-sized city. I took advantage of a national brand (CostCo) when I needed to have my eyes checked because of a sudden optical issue.

HEALTHCARE

Getting sick is not fun. When you are on the road and inside a small vehicle, it is tougher than in the comforts of your home. Like most things in vanlife, healthcare support is not absent, but may require searching for help, and more preparation to make it work.

Helpful vanlife healthcare tips:

- Be sure to carry all your insurance cards with you as you travel.

- Keep your prescriptions in the original refill bottles to help when refilling. Most U.S. drug plans let you use any pharmacy brand, but check your policy before traveling.

- Know your insurance coverage limitations before you travel, particularly if crossing national borders. Most U.S.-based clinics and hospitals accept valid health insurance policies, but it is best to check coverage before you need it.

- If you are traveling outside the U.S., talk to your insurance agent or provider before traveling. Most U.S. healthcare policies DO NOT cover service outside U.S. borders. There are exceptions and workarounds, and you can also buy traveler's health insurance to cover you in countries outside the U.S.

- If you use a home base (as I do), consider continuing to use your doctors there for your annual checkups and visits. This approach takes some planning, but unless you have a condition requiring frequent checkups, it is easy to coordinate annual or infrequent healthcare visits.

- Talk to your doctor about giving you a broad-spectrum antibiotic prescription to carry while traveling. Fill this before you leave home, because if you need this, you would rather have it immediately than trying to fill the prescription on the road. This came in handy for me when I got sick from a fast-acting salmonella episode, probably from new lettuce. Since I was staying at a Florida State Park, I was in no condition to drive and get the meds. Having the antibiotic with me shortened my suffering time. Be aware you should verify with your doctor or a medical professional whether your symptoms indicate a bacteria-based illness (where taking antibiotic will be helpful) or a viral one (where taking the antibiotic would waste the prescription).

- Take a good first-aid kit that contains at least some antibiotic cream, an assortment of bandages in various sizes, bandage wraps, finger splints, tapes, instant heat and cool packets, first-aid reference card, a tick pulling tool, etc. If you are planning to hike extensively in known poisonous snake country, having a snake-bite kit in your backpack is a good idea.

- Keep various extras in your vehicle: Ample prescriptions, spare eyeglasses, extra relief medications you have used before for inflammation, stomach issues, diarrhea, flu, cold, etc. While supplies are plentiful when traveling through towns, it always seems you need these when camping in the wild.

LAUNDRY

If you enjoyed the luxury of having your own washer/dryer in your home, then get ready for the fascinating cultural experience of a public, coin-operated laundromat! All kidding aside, these are easy to find in almost every town you will travel through. However, finding one that is clean and not full of people can be a challenge!

Tips to survive (and enjoy) a public laundromat:

- Arrange a specific place in your vehicle to store dirty clothes between laundromat visits. A tote with a lid or similar option is best to keep the smell of dirty clothes from overpowering your small living space.

- Plan on doing laundry every 7-10 days, seasonally dependent. Much longer than that and it becomes difficult to isolate dirty clothes and the odor.

- Keep a small pouch for quarters in your vehicle and whenever you get quarters in change, toss them in this pouch. Occasionally you will need to buy quarters, but laundromats usually have a change machine on site. TIP: Avoid using laundromats that have their own tokens or require you to use their own preloaded cards. Both cases can mean doing laundry there will cost you more, because you will probably never return to use your tokens or the credits left on a prepaid card.

- Carry your own laundry soap. I recommend the ease of using laundry pods: less mess, easier to store, simpler to use.

- Always do a sniff test on both washers and dryers before using them. In public laundromats, people wash and dry some odd things. Most laundromats either prohibit horse or dog blankets/bedding, or have units designated to use for these dirty, smelly laundry loads. You never know what the previous person tossed into a machine, but at least a sniff test helps you avoid the worst of these issues.

- If you have a large load of laundry, you can split into two dryers to save time.

- Remember, you only need to be inside the laundromat while loading the washer or dryer, or folding clothes. Staying in your van or vehicle lets you take care of some tasks, read, check stuff online, etc.

- Use your smartphone to time loads to minimize time in the laundromat.

- Some campgrounds have washer/dryers, but these take longer to use and sometimes you have to wait for them to be available.

- Most laundromats have a drop-off service where they will wash and fold for you and you pick your clean clothes up later.

MAIL

Full-time vanlifers usually need to create a new legal residency or domicile in a state friendly to full-time van and RVers. Along with this, you will probably want to set up a mail-forwarding service. I cover more about these issue in "Chapter 7: Personal Stuff – Challenges & Solutions, Mail," along with better options to receive packages while traveling.

Setting up most of your important mail to arrive via e-mail will help reduce how much goes to your forwarder, and thus reduce the cost of forwarding physical mail to you.

PETS

Those who travel with pets will tell you they are wonderful companions, whether alone or traveling with others. No question, the comfort of having pets with you takes away some of the loneliness, if that concerns you.

Vanlife with a dog or cat has a few different limitations. The primary one is that you cannot leave them in the vehicle in hot or cold weather. While they might previously have stayed home while you ran errands, your home had an automatic climate system to keep them safe. In a vehicle, it is more challenging to keep it cool or warm without expensive battery systems to run air conditioning, or automated heating while you are away from the vehicle. This will limit your hiking and outside activities, such as biking or kayaking. Although some areas allow dogs on hikes, more places do not (e.g., National Parks, an increasing number of state parks, some RV parks, etc.)

Some vanlifers solve this problem through expensive lithium battery systems to run air conditioners, or have propane or diesel heaters that run in the vehicle when the engine is off. These pet owners usually have vehicle temperature monitors they check via smartphones, with alerts if unsafe temperatures or system failures occur.

If you do go hiking and leave your pet(s) behind in your vehicle with adequate cooling or heating, be sure to leave a note on the window explaining this! Could avoid someone contacting authorities to do a save-the-pet window break-in.

I do not travel with a pet, although I have considered the idea. For me, the extra effort and limitations have kept me from taking a dog with me. I know more vanlifers who travel with a dog or cat than those who do not. Clearly, their pets are important to them and they think the limitations are acceptable for the reward. The pets seem to enjoy vanlife, although dogs more so than cats, in my experience talking with vanlifers traveling with pets. Regardless, if the benefits of having your pet with you are important to you, go for it.

Other Pet-related Concerns:

- Carry a copy of your pet's inoculation records if you plan to leave the U.S. and travel in Canada or Mexico.

- Access to emergency vet care is available in most cities and towns, and I have heard from other vanlifers that some vets may provide after-hour emergency care in places without an emergency vet clinic.

- Be aware that many campgrounds and parks enforce leash rules, and a violation usually means immediate campground expulsion.

- Carry enough special food with you, if your pet requires such, to last between visits to larger cities. Small towns will probably only stock the basic pet food brands.

SAFETY

As a solo, male traveler, I perceive personal safety as a minimal issue, whereas a solo, female traveler may have more concerns and situational needs. Is this perception true? Certainly, based on the number of YouTube videos about solo, female vanlife safety, it must be.

While I have no scientific data to say one way or the other, most of the solo female vanlifers I know do not think they are unsafe traveling in a van. Whether women's vanlife safety issues are over-hyped in the media, or women more adept at reading situations and avoiding personal safety risks, I do not know for sure.

Staying Nimble

Clearly one vanlife advantage, whether you are male or female, is that you are living in a box with wheels and an engine, and you can drive away from uncomfortable or potentially dangerous situations. While that does not cover all situations, it provides more reactionary *nimbleness* than staying in a hotel room.

Traveling solo safely requires *common sense* and *learning to recognize your body's warning signs* for uncomfortable things or situations. In my travels there were several times I stopped to overnight in a place, only to sense something was not right, then started the engine and drove off to elsewhere. There were no obvious signs that something was about to happen, but an uneasy sense and learned ability to listen to my body told me to drive on. This reaction requires paying attention (radio off, eyes and ears open, mind focused on how the body feels) for these clues to indicate you should go elsewhere.

The times I moved on were not just in undeveloped natural areas, but when stealth-camping on the street, or overnighting at places like Walmart or Cracker Barrel. Your best safety defense may be active situational awareness. Keep ego out of the way and, if uncomfortable, do not be dismissive, stubborn, or ignore the signs. A true rule of thumb in vanlife is it is okay to move on, because there is always another place just down the road.

SEASONAL NEEDS

Vanlife in summer sunshine has different needs than traveling during cold weather seasons. For full-timers, carrying things for all seasons is more challenging than for part-time vanlifers who travel by season. Full-timers typically go lightly in an all-season coverage approach, trying to take things that will layer to keep warm, or buy/dispose of some items after a season is over.

For many, though, simply chasing consistent seasons helps limit how much you need to prepare for. Many vanlifers travel south in the winter, then travel back north in the summer. This flow allows for easier adaptation than trying to live in weather extremes.

SHOWERING

Vanlife does not mean giving up showers, but likely means getting past the myth of needing to shower daily. At home, we take the convenience of a shower or bath for granted. On the road, a shower is a multi-step process that requires planning for time, weather, and location, whether you are showering in or behind your vehicle, or inside a pop-up camp cabana. When you are at a campground the process is much simpler to use their facilities.

As one ages, we realize daily showers are not necessary. Unless you are active in sports in hot weather, humans can easily go many days without showers, instead using wet wipes to clean underarms and private body areas daily.

This showering philosophy, along with using a toilet, is probably one of our learned behaviors that can be challenging to break. A vanlifer needs to overcome this myth of daily showers, else they will spend too much time refilling water or looking for public showers. If your rig has a built-in shower and toilet, and uses tanks to manage black and grey waste, that does not mean daily showers are a good idea. Part of successful vanlife travel is about managing on-board resources, and nothing uses up your water and fills your waste tank more than frequent showering.

Tips and tricks:

- Carry a pair of flip-flops to wear for safety from slipping and from catching foot-related fungus at public showers. I also take my bath towel and washcloth, although some facilities may supply towels.

- Join a fitness franchise to use their showers while traveling. I joined Anytime Fitness, whose locations are plentiful in the U.S. and Canada. Best of all, most have private shower rooms.

- Join Silver Sneakers (if over 65) and use their app to find one of their 13,000 U.S. facilities with showers to use.

- Use the showers available at campgrounds and RV parks. These are sometimes free or inexpensive coin-operated showers, and although not always super clean, can be a viable option.

- Look for community centers with coin-operated showers in small cities or towns, and public showers at a marina, if the town is near a lake.

- Pay to shower at truck stops along interstates or high-traffic highways. This is an especially convenient option if you decide to overnight there. These are not inexpensive (usually $10) but I have found they are usually clean and nice facilities.

- Use your internal shower if your RV has one (and use the military shower approach noted below), but be aware of moisture and condensation issues typical with these interior showers. Failing to control the rapid increase of humidity and moisture adequately when showering inside can lead to mildew and mold issues later, typically behind wall panels, etc.

- Use a pop-up cabana to create a shower behind your vehicle. The same cabana can also be a dressing room, toilet room, or extra storage not visible by others .

Setting up a shower off the back of your vehicle or at a campsite:

- Use a modesty curtain or tarp to create a private space off the back of your van or by stringing ropes across trees.

- Hang a camping solar shower (a device you fill with water and hang up in the sunshine to heat) off part of your van or a nearby tree. These units will get hot enough to shower within an hour or so.

- Use a portable shower head/pump with a bucket filled with cold water and a little boiled water (instead of a solar shower).

- Use a mat or raised boards to stand on during the shower.

Five-minute-or-less military shower technique to conserve water:

1. Turn water on, rinse quickly, then turn water off.
2. Lather up with soap everywhere needed (except hair).
3. Turn water on and quickly rinse, then turn water off.
4. Repeat the above two steps to wash hair when needed. Another myth exists that frequent hair shampooing (some think daily) is necessary; it is not.

Exotic shower options:

- Roof-rack-mounted pressurized shower tube: a water-filled black tube attached to a roof rack and pressurized with compressed air, then heated via solar exposure

- Propane-powered hot water unit using van or RV's internal pump-driven water system

TOILETING

Finding toilets on the road is easier than finding showers, but a vanlifer still needs a workable emergency toilet solution. Creating a vehicle-based solution means resolving the challenges of both liquid and solid waste in terms of storage, odor, and disposal. Without getting too graphic, separating the two waste types helps reduce odor, but takes extra effort.

Carry one or more of these toileting solutions:

- **Odor control** – I list this first, since it is fundamental to any of these options. Many chemical solutions exist for controlling waste odor and breaking down waste for easier disposal. My choice for the various setups I have tried is Happy Camper, an organic powder compound for both liquid and solid waste, and, if in use, both grey and black waste tanks.

- **Hard core** – A common, home-improvement type, five-gallon plastic bucket with a plastic bag to contain waste for later disposal in a trash dumpster. An optional bucket-top seat makes this option slightly more civilized.

- **Soft core** – Thetford makes a line of porta-potties that are a step up from pooping in a bucket, but you are still pooping in a *refined* bucket. These have waste units you disconnect from the sitting unit to carry to a typical campground or RV dump facility, or directly to an indoor toilet. They have a sliding gate that helps keep odor out and an inboard clean water reservoir used for rinsing the toilet bowl. Emptying can be a frequent task unless you buy one of their larger units. Dumping can be in a rest room or at a RV dump station.

- **Civilized soft core** – Onboard cassette toilet, like those found in Class B RVs. Similar to a Thetford porta-potti, except permanently installed and the cassette removed from outside the van. Dumping can be in a rest room or at a RV dump station.

- **Decadent** – Onboard toilet hooked to onboard black tank. Emptying the tank is via a connecter outside the vehicle and a dump hose stored somewhere in the van or underneath. Requires a designated RV waste dump facility.

- **Compostable toilets** – Usually an installed toilet (expensive), or homemade version. Installed versions usually have a small 12-volt fan exhausted to the outside. Solid waste mixes with compost material (pine chips, coconut shreds, etc.) and then goes into a bag for disposal in a trash dumpster. Liquid waste goes into a separate container and is poured into a toilet or RV dump site. The solid waste in this type of toilet composts enough to control odor, but not enough to spread into soil, thus requires tossing into a waste dumpster or container.

- **Backpacker style** – Small hole dug about a foot deep, then covered after use. This is old school, but allowable in wild forested land (although watch for signs; some places this is a prohibited practice).

My current camper van solution is finding restrooms for solid waste, although I carry a Stansport portable toilet (basically a bucket with a seat and a plastic bag) for emergencies and use bag liners with a solidifying/odor agent inside (later tossing into a trash dumpster). Liquid waste goes into my converted grey tank via a male urinal cup attached to a hose going into the grey tank. I prime the tank with Happy Camper powder each time I empty the tank, then when full, dump the grey tank at a RV dump station.

VACATION MODE

Oh, the thrill of vanlife when you first roll off down the road traveling to new adventures! All of us who start traveling vanlife go through an initial stage called "vacation mode," loosely defined as doing and visiting anything you want, accompanied by eating and drinking anything you would like. Much like how we behave on a typical vacation break, vanlife vacation mode is a blast, so why not? You earned it by taking the leap to change your lifestyle to this freer, nomadic way of living.

Nothing wrong with vacation mode... unless you cannot make it stop to finally start normal-living mode. This transition away from vacation mode is necessary, since your monthly budget most likely cannot continue supporting vacation mode. It is not uncommon to run a month or so in vacation mode, then realize it is time to taper off and into a daily routine. This does not mean you stop visiting awesome places or museums across the country, but means you settle into more of a routine and live within a budget, allowing for some fun here and there.

CHAPTER 8
THE #1 QUESTION:
DO YOU GET LONELY?

Traveling alone doesn't always mean you're alone. Most often, you meet marvelous people along the way and make connections that last a lifetime.

JACQUELINE BOONE

Traveling around the country in a van or other vehicle can be inspiring. There are a lot of opportunities for quiet, contemplative moments, whether you are hiking solo in nature, or enjoying a peaceful, early-morning campsite by yourself with a cup of hot coffee. But not everyone is comfortable being alone, without travel companions or socializing. How vanlifers handle solitude can make life on the road happy and fulfilling, or somewhat miserable.

BEING ALONE VERSUS LONELINESS

The most frequent question I am asked is: "Do you get lonely traveling alone?" My answer is always no, but I am aware loneliness is something people can struggle with. Others, like my introverted self, embrace solitude and tend to thrive in that environment. "Do you get lonely?" is an important question, to which you should know your answer if you are considering vanlife, especially solo traveling.

There are differences between being alone and loneliness. Being alone is a state of being, meaning you are by yourself, and thus in control of your options and decisions. Being alone can certainly lead to loneliness, but some people can find themselves lonely in a relationship, or around others. Loneliness is sadness about being disconnected from others. Thus, those who are alone without feeling loneliness probably have connected well with themselves.

Some people assume introverts avoid loneliness and company. Extroverts and introverts both need connections, but introverts are happiest when connections are by their choice and infrequent. A solo vanlife introvert may be fine connecting with others online to avoid loneliness, or meeting friends occasionally on the road. Extroverts, however, most likely need a lot of online and in-person connections.

POWER OF SOLITUDE

For those who embrace solitude, there are significant benefits:

- Improve creativity
- Improve mental wellbeing
- Learn one's self better; become more comfortable with you
- Find your own voice, e.g., opinions, values, writing, confidence
- Improve mindfulness
- Heighten awareness of nature

Annual Reflective Retreats

Many people do an annual solo retreat: a week or two somewhere isolated, in nature, and for the most part unplugged from devices. Bill Gates does this to reflect, think, create, and unplug from our wired world. For years, I have gone on mini-retreats that lasted at least a weekend, if not longer. I find somewhere in nature conducive to reflecting on my past year and considering plans for the next year. I leave my cell phone and laptop in the car and go through this process analog style: pencil and yellow legal pads. The time spent alone in this environment, doing this process, helps me focus and think more deeply.

> We cannot change what we are not aware of, and once we are aware, we cannot help but change.
>
> SHERYL SANDBERG

If you are interested in learning more about solitude and its benefits, see "Appendix B – Resources & Links" for a booklist on solitude.

SOLO TRAVELERS

Many vanlifers (if not most, based on my circle of vanlife friends) are solo travelers, and most are women. Couples travel together, of course, so I am not saying vanlife is best-suited for solo travelers, but it works well for those who embrace solitude and the benefits of being alone. Many solo vanlifers I know travel with pets, which perhaps helps them mitigate any residual loneliness.

One benefit of vanlife that appeals to solo travelers is having control of where you go and what you do. Deciding on these things as a solo traveler is less stressful than needing to agree with another person on where, when, and what.

Having the full space in your vehicle just for you is another perk of solo vanlife. You get to decide what to take, how to store it, and how you organize your vehicle overall.

As for me and many solo travelers I know, we are active in some creative pursuit, whether writing, art, music, etc. Some continue to work full-time from their vans, so their work becomes a solitary pursuit, although they are likely connected to other online.

I see my vanlife as traveling in a mobile writer's studio, equipped with what I need for my writing projects. Camping in inspirational places is conducive to my writing. I can connect when necessary to the internet for research, blogging, publishing, and connecting with others.

In pre-COVID-19 days, whether at home or traveling, I spent much of my time "camped" out in a coffee shop somewhere, writing or journaling. I loved the white noise of coffee shop ambiance, and of course, with someone else making my java and tempting me with a tasty nosh or two (cookies and muffins were and are my weakness). These days, I spend most of my creative time inside the van or at a campsite, staying away from public places to reduce COVID-19 risks. I do look forward to when I can resume my much-beloved practice of coffee shop writing.

You may gain more clarity on this subject (and my perspective) by watching my YouTube video, Solo Traveler – Loneliness?

TWO OR MORE TRAVELERS

When two or more people take to the road, space seems squeezed and often means there is no place for private time. Depending on the weather, one solution is to pull over at a rest area or park and let the person who needs space get out and walk. But often this option is not available, and a pair may have to deal with stress and tension until emotions settle or they find an opportunity to stop.

There is a saying in vanlife that you will know how good your marriage is after two weeks of traveling together in a van. Travelers who are physically active and do outside sports can offset the space issues, but I know many other traveling couples who are fairly sedentary, and still get along fine traveling in a small, rolling home. The people involved determine whether they can happily co-exist, or be better off as solo travelers. Often, newcomers to vanlife will not know how they will co-exist until after a few weeks on the road.

I admire and am amazed by couples who not only travel together, but with kids! I know some who are doing this full-time, which to me is even more amazing. These travelers are examples of what happens when everyone traveling supports living and cooperating in a small space.

CONCLUSION

If you are an introvert and engaged in some type of creative pursuit or enjoy immersion in nature, then you should be okay with the solitude, and rarely experience loneliness. If this description does not fit you, you can probably manage being alone and the potential for loneliness by developing a greater awareness of your emotions, and learning how to adjust your thinking and perception.

Handling loneliness is not a simple task. If you sometimes deal with loneliness, yet still want to get into vanlife, then you might consider talking to a professional on what might work for you. My opinions, suggestions and perspective are from my experiences of talking to others, knowing myself, and a lot of reading on the subjects. Hopefully, this chapter helps you, but *does not replace seeking professional help* if you need to learn how to handle being alone and loneliness during your vanlife experience.

CHAPTER 9
VEHICLE STUFF – CHALLENGES & SOLUTIONS

> Take care of your car in the garage, and the car will take care of you on the road.

AMIT KALANTRI

Regardless of which vehicle you choose for vanlife, and whether it is new or used, keeping up with repairs and maintenance makes traveling safer and more carefree. Think of this vehicle as your home on wheels; you would not ignore or delay repairs and maintenance on your home, so take care of things proactively when something needs repair or replacement.

BREAKING DOWN OR GETTING STUCK

If your vehicle gets a flat tire or breaks down, and you have to pull over to the side of the road and wait for help, this can be a stressful and uncomfortable situation. In your home on wheels, at least you have comfort and supplies while you wait. Events like this rarely happen in convenient locations, often in a remote area, at night, or any combination.

Getting at least one (two are better) roadside assistance service can ease your mind if you need help. Paying for roadside service is an easy (and wise) decision in vanlife, along with other proactive steps to help with vehicle challenges:

- *Check your vehicle insurance options* for roadside service with your policy, and then choose another plan from Coach Net, Good Sam, or others. Compared to passenger car roadside service, RV-specific (which would include vans) roadside service is broader, and usually extends farther off paved roads. Policies and conditions vary, so read the details carefully.

- *Carry a spare tire.* Not every vanlifer agrees this is necessary. Statistically, close to 90% of flat tires are repairable with a patch kit, which you should carry. The other 10% are sidewall damage or tread separation (neither are roadside repairable). With these two types of tire failures, having a spare tire could get you back on the road quickly. Without a spare, a tow is necessary to a tire shop. Depending on your tire brand and size, finding a tire shop that has yours in stock may be difficult. This may strand you until the shop can get a matching tire delivered, and may mean renting a hotel room if the tire shop will not let you overnight in their parking lot.

Whether or not to carry a spare tire depends on several factors:

- Does your vehicle come with a **spare tire**, or can you adapt it to carry one? While you may elect to stow a tire inside a vehicle such as a van, rubber tires smell bad, besides taking up valuable space.

- What is your **risk-aversion level** and how much peace of mind do you need for a low-probability event?

- Can you **physically handle changing a tire** on your vehicle? Note that having a spare does not mean you should avoid buying a roadside service policy. On larger vehicles, changing the spare yourself is usually not a good idea because of weight, bulk, and jacking conditions.

- Where are you **planning to travel**? If towns are not far away, perhaps a spare is unnecessary. If you are going to more desolate places, like Alaska or Mexico, then I recommend traveling with a spare tire.

Equip your vehicle to handle getting stuck. Those with vehicles outfitted for dirt roads run a higher risk of getting stuck in sand, mud, or rough terrain. New drivers can easily get excited while traveling these areas and take their vehicles places they should not. There are specific techniques and specialized equipment to carry that might free your rig by your own efforts, so you do not have to rely on being found by someone who can pull you out of trouble:

- *Know your driving skill and rig limitations* – Those of us who love to drive into the wild can get excited about forging down a dirt path, and will often take our homes on wheels into places with risks of getting stuck. Best to know your limits (ground clearance, drivetrain, shocks/struts, tire types, etc.) and learn your vehicle's features that could help navigate difficult conditions (traction controls, gearing, gear lockers, weight ratios, etc.). The best approach for some may simply be conservative common sense.

- *Airing down tires* – If you are stuck in loose dirt or sand, dropping the air pressure in a tire to about half of normal creates broader tire treads, which add more surface area and thus may get you unstuck. Many people who travel in ground conditions where this helps drop the tire air pressures to travel even before getting stuck. They usually carry a 12-volt air compressor to air back up afterward. If you do not have an air compressor in your rig, airing down may still get you unstuck, but then you risk damaging your tire if you cannot air back up before you get back onto pavement.

- *Good shovel* – Many drivers carry a full-length shovel on a roof rack or a fold-up type hand shovel. Either is good to dig out a stuck tire (a common situation). Sometimes that alone will get you moving, but you may need to combine shoveling with other equipment.

- *Recovery boards* – Vanlifers driving in the wild usually carry a pair of recovery boards. These go under a tire after shoveling out dirt or mud and can provide enough traction to drive out of the problem. Boards can either be full-size, which are transported strapped to a roof rack or van's back door ladder, or a folding type (what I have and use), stowed inside the vehicle.

- *Wait for a good Samaritan* – Off-roaders are typically generous with helping stranded vanlifers. The price you pay for this option is waiting for someone to happen along and find you stranded. Sometimes you may have to walk out from where you are stuck to find help. Note in these situations, roadside service is probably not going to help you since you may be too far off a paved road for their service.

FUEL COSTS

Once you shift from houselife to vanlife, unless you have a large vehicle payment to the bank, your major monthly expense is probably going to be the fuel that gets you down the road. Whether this is gasoline or diesel, and what vehicle you chose, nursing your vehicle's mpg may be a new skill you need.

If your vehicle's mpg makes your fuel budget larger than you would like, there are two options to consider: driving less, or driving slower. With most vehicles, the mpg gained by dropping from an average 70 mph speed to 55 or 60 can be substantial, resulting in lower cost per mile and extending driving range before needing to fill up.

Initially, you can expect your monthly fuel costs to be high as you settle into a routine and get past the excitement of new travels. You will learn how to pace the miles over the month to keep the fuel costs as reasonable as possible.

You may also want to become a savvy fuel shopper. There are significant price differences between fuel brands and stations locations, such as stations on major highways and those farther off the exit ramp. Experience with driving different areas will help you learn these differences, but the smartphone app GasBuddy can help. The app shows you current prices for stations near you, or near a location you enter. These prices come from users of the app reporting prices as they drive and fill up. GasBuddy has a huge base of users, and the information is usually fairly current and reliable. Google Maps will also show you station prices in search results, which you can access by using Google Maps as your GPS navigator and searching for "gas stations near me" or "gas stations on my route."

Note that when fuel prices are high, driving extra miles may not save per gallon: the per-mile cost of fuel to get to that lower priced station could negate the per-gallon savings.

Shopping club membership stores such as CostCo and Good Sam can give you deep discounts on gasoline prices, although these places usually do not have diesel. On last year's trip on the West Coast, I saved significantly (sometimes 20% or more) using CostCo to fill up. Other big box stores like Walmart and major grocery chains sometimes have service stations with prices lower than the area's branded stations. These other places will appear in apps like GasBuddy.

My approach when traveling is to fill up when my fuel gauge shows a quarter tank left. This approach reduces the risk of running out of fuel, although depends on where you travel. I have traveled where stations were a hundred miles or more apart, so the quarter tank option for my vehicle would be too close for my comfort. Situational awareness should guide you when to refuel.

Some vanlifers carry extra gas, particularly those in camper vans or RV. On my Travato, I mounted a RotopaX two-gallon gas container on the rear door. This option is especially a good idea if you plan to travel in remote places. If you opt for carrying extra gas, be sure to mount it on the exterior of your vehicle in a place safe from possible impact.

MAINTENANCE

Keep a log of repairs and maintenance to track repeating items such as oil changes, tire rotations, etc. I recommend you at least follow the manufacturer's maintenance schedule, especially if your vehicle is new or fairly new, since warranty work depends on compliance with that schedule.

- Oil and filter changes should be per your vehicle/engine's recommended intervals, and not necessarily the oil service place's suggestion. These do not have to be at a dealership, but you can use specialty oil and lube place such as the Valvoline, Jiffy Lube, etc. These locations are usually less expensive than dealerships, and often more convenient.

- Change your air filter at the recommended intervals, or sooner if you drive a lot of dusty dirt roads.

- Change your cabin air filter at the recommended intervals to keep your inside cabin air exchange clean, sooner if you drive a lot of dusty dirt roads.

- Rotate tires per your vehicle's user manual recommendation. Changing oil and rotating tires at the same time is a good idea to help you remember to do both consistently, especially if your vehicle uses synthetic oil, which does not require changing as frequently.

- Follow your recommended service intervals in the vehicle's maintenance manual. This is especially important with a new vehicle for the first 100,000 miles to keep your mechanicals working to manufacturer's specifications.

- Periodically (perhaps every 3,000-to-5,000 miles) go through your van and tighten nuts and bolts on your cabin buildouts, or when you notice a new rattle or squeak. Waiting to do so may cause more significant repairs, since vibrating pieces can break other pieces if not fixed early.

- Periodically deep clean your vehicle (meaning removing most everything), which also gives you an opportunity to inspect and fix issues early.

- If you have solar panels on your vehicle's roof, periodically clean them. As the panels get dirty, their solar efficiency declines, although the difference in captured energy is not significant unless the panels are really dirty. Carry a short-handle extendable tool with a soft cleaning element, plus a rubber squeegee strip to use with a spray water bottle to clean the panels. If your vehicle's roof is hard to reach, consider carrying a collapsible ladder to make this task easier. The ladder is also helpful if you need to inspect your roof after severe weather, or after driving under low tree limbs and hearing them bounce off your vehicle's roof!

REPAIR

Living in your vehicle makes it your home. You would not ignore a necessary repair to your home, so repair your vehicle when needed. Being proactive and doing recommended preventive maintenance can help avoid or lessen breakdown severity.

During preventative maintenance visits, ask the facility to inspect your vehicle's belts, fluids, suspension, and tires, even if not included per your vehicle's preventive maintenance interval. Proactively replacing a part you know will wear out soon avoids surprises and provides peace of mind.

SEASONAL & WEATHER

If you travel full-time, then you need to carry the right clothing for summer and winter. Traveling with seasons minimizes this need somewhat, but there are other seasonal and weather exposures you should consider:

- Learn to be vigilant of current and forecasted weather for where you are or where you are going. While you are mobile and can move easily if needed, failure to study weather forecasts on the route over the next several days can expose you to serious situations, both in driving safety and the potential for stranding or vehicle damage.

- When camping in the wild (or even at organized campsites and parks), be aware of ground conditions and proximities to rivers, creeks, or arroyos. If significant rain is forecasted, or during that area's rain or winter weather season, use extra caution.

- Use weather forecasts and apps to know about potential high-wind conditions, especially if in a high-top van or larger RV. In winds topping 60 mph, driving a mini-van is not fun and could be dangerous. See "Appendix B – Resources & Links" for recommendations.

- Even if the weather looks good, pay attention to roads and campsites for signs of problems when it gets wet, such as erosion, lots of dried-mud ruts, soil or vegetation that appears moved from rushing surface water, etc.

- If you camp during high winds, determine which direction the wind is blowing and use the sailor's trick: point your "land yacht" into the teeth of the wind. This will not eliminate rocking and buffeting of your vehicle, but it will significantly lessen it and reduce wind damage risk.

STORING VEHICLES WHEN TRAVELING ELSEWHERE

Sometimes during vanlife, you may need to leave your vehicle and travel via air, train, or bus to somewhere else. Maybe you have a wedding or funeral to attend, or simply an extra, traditional vacation you take in between vanlife. The challenge of where to leave your home on wheels becomes magnified when you realize it contains your worldly possessions and you are abandoning it for a week, a month, or more. Fortunately, others before you faced this dilemma and discovered many solutions that work.

Whichever method you choose, take most of your electronics (phone, laptop, iPad, etc.) with you. Store electronics you cannot take somewhere other than your vehicle if possible. Also remove your secret stash box and take the contents with you or store outside the vehicle, possibly with a friend or family member.

Temporary storage location tips and techniques:

General

- Keep anything valuable out of sight should someone look in a window. This means even minor items, such as pocket change in a cup holder. Nothing loose should be visible.

- Choose a good and secure storage location partly based on whether your vehicle blends in. The plainer your vehicle, the better your chances of avoiding issues.

- Put coverings inside your windows to block outside viewers. Thieves need to work quickly, so many may pass on a vehicle they cannot see inside. This logic is, of course, random and unpredictable, but probably better to do this than take chances.

- Use cab privacy curtains in your van vehicle to block seeing past the cab/front seats. Doing so shows there is nothing to steal in the front, plus helps your vehicle look more like a work van or basic passenger car than a nomadic home full of stuff.

- Fill your gas tank before parking in cold weather to avoid freezing condensation in the fuel tank, making engine-starting troublesome. Adding a locking fuel cap is probably a good idea.

- Batteries, both coach and chassis, are not usually a concern for short-term absences of less than a month. Beyond that, you might install a solar trickle charger for your engine battery. If you have roof-mounted solar panels charging your coach batteries, they should be fine. Longer-term storage may mean shutting off your coach battery system or disconnecting the batteries, but there are a lot of factors that determine whether this is a good idea. If you are storing your vehicle much longer than a month, do some research to figure out which method is best in your situation.

- Use or dispose of food in your refrigerator or cooler before storing the vehicle for more than a week or two. If you have a power issue and your refrigerator loses power, the food inside will spoil quickly and the resulting smell in the refrigerator is difficult to remove.

Airport Hotel

Many hotels will allow travelers to leave their vehicles parked in their lot while they travel, but that may require staying there at least one night. Safety varies by location and the hotel's commitment to parking lot security. Some hotels charge for parking, but many let you park free.

Airport Parking

Use long-term parking because it is in an uncovered, open, and highly visible area, and likely more patrolled by private security. Choose a parking spot closer to where there is more daily traffic.

Boondockers Welcome Host

This is a RV-only club where private hosts let RVers stay for free. I have heard it might be possible to store a member's RV at one of these host's houses while traveling, but this depends on a host's setup. Some may ask for a small fee, but this option might be worth looking into if you have the membership.

Friends/Relative's House

Possibly the best option, but highly dependent on your host's diligence and willingness to check on your vehicle frequently, and what the location provides in parking and security. It is a bonus if your friend or relation can start and briefly drive your vehicle every week to keep batteries charged and fluids moving. The perfect solution is a friend or relative with available garage space that fits your vehicle.

RV Dealer

The RV dealer where you purchased your RV may allow you to park there while you travel. It might be worth asking a nearby RV dealer, even if you did not purchase from them.

Storage Facility

This can be a local RV-focused storage lot, or a typical storage facility with room for vehicles. The challenge is finding one with short-term space; most only rent vehicle storage spots by the month or longer. Security is often just a fence versus a patrol, so if you have a vehicle fire or theft, it may be days or weeks before the facility notices.

Taking It With You

An exotic option for some, but perhaps viable in certain situations, is to truck or ship your vehicle to your destination. Obvious pluses includes having the vehicle to use while there, lowering hotel costs, etc. Transportation cost can be quite high, and timing is a challenge.

I traveled to Hawaii for a month and stored my Travato Class B RV at a friend-of-a-friend's place north of Denver, Colorado. Before committing to that, I checked out transporting my RV to Hawaii. The cheapest cost to do this in 2019 was $3,500, but at that price, I would need to leave the van with the shipper *three weeks* before departure. There would be another three-week window for the company to make the van available after I returned. These unpredictable waits were a deal-killer for me, since I was full-time living in the van. As I discovered, taking the Travato there was not a good idea: narrow roads, constant heavy traffic, and rare is a level parking spot!

TRAVELING OUTSIDE THE U.S.

I have yet to leave the continental U.S. during my vanlife years, but each year I hope to wander up in Canada. Unfortunately, the pandemic prevented this, but it is on my list once it is safe to cross the border. Some vanlifers really enjoy traveling to Mexico. If that is your desire, be aware there are more concerns going south from the U.S. than going north.

Traveling to either country has specific limitations and issues, so be sure to research those deeply via Google or YouTube.

Tips, tricks, and cautions traveling to Canada or Mexico:

Cell Service

Both countries require different network connections or data roaming enabled if you want to use your cell phone or connect to the internet. Research both before going so you can change your cell phone plan or add extra equipment.

Food

Both countries restrict what food you may take in (or bring back). Check specifics before you cross the border. Eating locally is a major concern in Mexico.

Healthcare

Crossing the U.S. border usually means your U.S. healthcare coverage will not apply or has significant limitations. Research with your health-care policy providers to know these limits, and/or consider buying traveler's health insurance that will work in the country you are visiting.

Mexico Specific

- Having someone in the vehicle who speaks Spanish is a good idea. Some travelers do without a fluent traveler on board, but being Spanish-deficient on a trip to Mexico adds potential difficulty to an already challenging travel situation.

- Drinking water is a health issue in Mexico, so prepare to only drink bottled water. You will not be able to continue the usual practice of filling your onboard water tanks for cooking or ingesting.

- Consider asking your doctor pre-trip for medications to help lessen symptoms should you develop intestinal issues via the local water or food.

Passport

Make sure yours is still valid and will not expire while in either country. Do not rely on just using your U.S. driver's license for crossing the border or identification while in the country. Should you need U.S. embassy help, you will need your passport.

Pets

Traveling with pets is more difficult. Be sure to take a copy of their medical records, since these are necessary when crossing borders.

Recreational/Medical Drugs

Be sure where you travel accepts your recreational drugs, or leave them at home. Take prescription drugs in the original bottles so there is no question what those pills are.

Time In Country

Another critical aspect to research is the limits on staying for both countries. Both have generous timeframes, but if you want or need to extend your visit, make sure you understand and know the limits. Staying past that end date could have severe consequences.

Vehicle Insurance

Your current vehicle insurance policy may or may not provide adequate coverage. Research insurance riders to add to your existing policy, or purchase separate insurance to meet each country's requirements.

Weapons

Do not take weapons to Canada or Mexico. If caught, consequences can mean extended jail time, depending on the severity of the offense.

WARRANTY WORK

New vehicles have manufacturer warranties. You should be aware of the limits of these warranties listed in your vehicle manuals so you know when they expire.

Recommendations:

- Keep a list of little things that need warranty work so you can stop by a dealership and take care of them when it is convenient. This is especially important with a new camper van or RV, since their warranty periods are typically short, e.g., 12 months or 15,000 miles.

- Plan to visit your RV dealer *just before the **earlier** of these two limitations expires* to take care of everything that needs warranty repair or is no longer fitting well, including things such as warped cabinet doors, faulty window coverings, etc.

Any equipment or appliance in a camper van or RV (even used ones), have separate warranties that typically last longer than camper van or RV warranties.

When purchasing a new camper van or RV, experienced RVers recommend avoiding the extended warranty. These are exceedingly expensive, and only cover the non-equipment manufacturer parts and accessories. They primarily are cash windfalls for the dealerships. A better option is to put that excessive fee amount into a personal fund to take care of any maintenance issues past the normal vehicle warranty. Most new camper van or RV owners find that issues will occur within the first year of ownership under the original warranty coverage.

CHAPTER 10
RESOURCES:
LIFEBLOOD OF VANLIFE

> Living with only the bare essentials has not only provided superficial benefits such as the pleasure of a tidy room or the simple ease of cleaning, it has also led to a more fundamental shift. It's given me a chance to think about what it really means to be happy.
>
> FUMIO SASAKI

While managing and replenishing resources for your vehicle may seem like a straight-forward, simple task, this sometimes becomes challenging during vanlife. Using the conveniences and accessories you have in your vehicle (air conditioning, heat, fan venting, etc.) contribute to resource consumption, forcing you to make choices about when to use them.

The tips, guidelines, and practices below for your vehicle's life-supporting resources will help with this challenge.

AIR CONDITIONING, HEATERS, FANS

Even though your vehicle normally provides all three, realistically they are only available while driving. You can run them by idling your vehicle at a campsite, but unless it is an emergency, that is not a good option, and it consumes fuel.

So, what happens when you stop at a campsite for days or weeks? You need to provide these comforts independent from your vehicle's systems.

Air Conditioning (A/C)

Typically, most motorized RVs or trailers include A/C. While installing an air conditioner in your DIY van or other vehicle is not a simple task, it is doable. The main challenges are wiring and powering the air conditioner, whether setting up for shore power, or through an advanced system of multiple lithium batteries. Typical RV or van AGM batteries will *not* power A/C.

Many vanlifers choose to avoid A/C because of the expense for the unit and the need for installing a sufficient electrical power system. However, those who travel with pets often need an A/C solution. Some purchase RVs or vans with lithium power systems and secondary, alternator recharging systems to provide on-demand cooling for their pets.

Heaters

Even if you travel carefully with the seasons, you may still experience nights or days where you need some heat. Turning on your vehicle for short periods to provide heat can be done, but this is not good long-term for your engine, and can be unsafe due to the possibility of engine exhaust fume poisoning. You may choose to carry a lot of blankets and tough it out. The best option is to install a separate heating solution for the area of your vehicle where you live and sleep, using one of these methods:

Portable Propane Heaters

- Many vanlifers start out with a Mr. Buddy or other small, inexpensive propane heater. These do work and keep you warm, but they have downsides and you should eventually replace them with something safer, more efficient on fuel, and a better heating source. They require a small propane tank to work, one that should not be in the vehicle while the heater is running. Venting the vehicle via roof fan or open window is a safety requirement, to avoid breathing any unburned propane. These heaters also provide a moist heat, which some find uncomfortable, and can easily introduce problematic amounts of humidity into the vehicle.

Built-in Propane Heaters

- A heater installed inside a closed cabinet and powered by a propane tank. Tanks are typically installed under the vehicle, but may be inside if in a sealed and outside-vented cabinet. Propane heaters typically provide heat through hoses and outlets in the vehicle, but can be wall-mounted, with a single intake/outflow. Typically found in many RVs, these heater types are inexpensive and usually reliable. Propane is an efficient gas and a tank can usually last a month when used for moderate heating and cooking.

Built-in Gas or Diesel Heaters

- These vehicle-fuel heaters are expensive, but they are the optimum choice for heating a rolling home. Consisting of a heater unit housed in an enclosed cabinet or underneath the van, they vent to the outside and provide dry-heated air via a duct system and outlets. Fuel for the heaters comes via tapping into the vehicle's fuel tank. Some commercial vans have a factory-installed fuel line tap, but other vehicles may require a professional mechanic to install the tap connection.

- These heaters are convenient since they use your vehicle fuel, which eliminates propane refills. To ensure enough fuel remains to avoid stranding, a shut-off system activates when the vehicle's fuel tank is a quarter full. With these vehicle-fuel heaters, you should fill your vehicle's tank if you expect to use the heater while stationary for several days.

- Units from reputable brands, such as Webasto or Planar are expensive, but reliable. Installation of this type of system is also expensive, and can run more than the cost of the unit. Like the inverters mentioned later, there are inexpensive gas/diesel heaters available, but based on reviews, these are less reliable and not recommended.

- These heaters require frequent, high heat runs to burn off accumulated carbon deposits. Most vehicles should use the 2 kilowatt units that will run hotter, reducing the frequency of carbon-deposit burn-off. Some DIYers opt for the 5 kilowatt units, but find they are oversized for the space, and thus never get hot enough to keep up with carbon deposit burn-off, leading to reliability issues.

Vent Fans

Many vanlifers use MaxxAir fans or similar roof-installed models to help vent coach areas. Some owners choose to install one fan fore and one fan aft to maximize air movement, especially on warm nights. Opening windows gives these fans some intake air to pull in and out, thus cooling the area. For this to work, windows need bug-proof screening, and, ideally, no-see-um proof. If you are DIYing a cargo van, you can choose windows to install with built-in screens.

If you use a propane cooktop while cooking inside your vehicle, you will need to properly vent the coach area. A roof-top fan combined with an open window near the cooktop makes this easier and safer.

ELECTRICAL

12-volt Power

- Electric power provided from your vehicle's chassis battery or the batteries you add for the vehicle's coach or living area is 12-volt power. Lights, fans, USB outlets, and any other electrical item running off the batteries needs to be 12-volt compatible.

- Wire 12-volt lights and equipment to a secondary battery(s), known as a coach battery. *Do not wire these added items to your vehicle's chassis battery/electrical system.* This could drain your engine's battery, and thus unable to start your vehicle's engine when needed.

- Alternately, you can use a portable power unit, such as a Jackery solar generator, to power things without special wiring.

- Learn 12-volt wiring techniques if you want to do it yourself and are handy with tools. If you choose DIY wiring, invest in good wiring tools: a wire stripper/cutter, connection crimper, 12-volt test light, and a power meter.

- Avoid the DIY option when wiring connections to the battery or installing hubs for multiple 12-volt connections. Unless you have 12-volt electrical experience, hire a pro for these needs.

- Be consistent in how you wire things. Use same color wires for hot side (powered) and for ground (black wire, typically and often labeled common); always use single wire runs (i.e., never splice two wires to make a long wire run); use heat-shrink shielded (covered) female or male connectors; use heat-shrink wrap over soldered joints; and zip-tie bundles of wires for a neater installation that is easier to troubleshoot and fix later.

- Spend time watching YouTube how-to 12-volt electrical videos before deciding on how/what/where to wire anything.

12-volt for Propane Heater/Cooktop

Depending on what kind of heater you install, other than a portable type, you may need to provide 12-volt power for its fan motor and igniter. These should be hard-wired in, and not powered via a Jackery, etc. Wire a large heater to a fuse box, or use a line fuse for a small one. A propane cooktop's igniter draws little power, so this does not need to be wired off shore power.

12-volt Coach Battery Systems

Typically, one or two 12-volt batteries will power most, if not all, of your 12-volt power coach or living area needs. Battery locations are usually underneath a vehicle, or inside the vehicle in a box or cabinet enclosure.

System may include:

- Wiring and plug to connect to shore power

- Wiring in a shore-powered battery charger

- A 12-volt fuse block to help protect 12-volt items and provide a central fuse point rather than inline fuses on each item

- Connection to chassis alternator wiring/relay/other for charging while driving

- Other miscellaneous electrical parts

AGM Battery

The AGM (Absorbed Glass Mat) lead-acid battery is the workhorse of the RV industry, and designed to hold deep charges and deliver more power on demand than a traditional, automotive-grade lead-acid battery, which work in situations that need a burst of starting power and only light use of 12-volt power when the engine is off. Vanlife coach buildouts should use AGM (or better) batteries and not automotive-grade lead-acid batteries.

Features and tips:

- Cost more than automotive lead-acid batteries, but less than lithium batteries.

- Provide ample power for vanlife *basic* needs within their safe usage zone.

- Can sustain damage if allowed to drop below 80% of full charge (this damage occurs from calcification of battery cells, which is usually reversible the first few times, but eventually the battery will no longer be fully rechargeable and may not provide enough power).

- Will work with plug-in battery chargers, alternator-connected charging, or solar charging.

- Are typically 100 amp hour (ah) batteries, but higher ah batteries are available.

- Install a battery monitor to check voltage and help avoid damaging batteries from letting them drop below their safe 80% level.

- Power a basic setup of lights, USB plugs, fans with one 100 ah AGM, but not a 12-volt refrigerator. To include running a 12-volt refrigerator, two AGM batteries are necessary.

- Not recommended to use an inverter powering off an AGM to run small 110-volt appliances, because of risk of dropping below 80% quickly, thus damaging the battery.

Lithium Batteries

More RVs and vans are using lithium batteries and, as prices drop, they will probably become the workhorse battery for RVs and van builds. Lithium batteries are superior to AGM batteries mostly because they provide more *available* power per battery than an AGM. With AGMs, only 20% of the battery is ideally usable before recharging, whereas lithiums can usually use up to 90% of the charge before recharging. This means two 100ah lithiums in a van compared to two 100ah AGMs provide roughly 5x the available power before recharging.

Features and tips:

- Cost more than AGMs (typically more than double), but prices are dropping as lithium technology improves and demand increases. Avoid the cheap lithiums from overseas unless a reputable expert (Will Prowse, etc.) reviews them in their YouTubes and states they are good.

- Requires a lithium-capable charger, both for shore-power or solar charging.

- Need protection from low temperatures. When below freezing, their energy is still usable, but lithium batteries will not recharge until the battery cores warm up above freezing. Thus, many lithium battery installations are inside the vehicle, or underneath in an enclosure supplied with heat. Some battery models now on the market are self-heating. I have two of these installed under my van. Last winter, although it was 5 degrees outside at night, the self-heating lithiums provided energy and were recharging despite being unprotected from temperatures.

- Will work with lithium-specific plug-in battery chargers, vehicle alternator charging during driving, solar charging via lithium-enabled solar charger, and shore power via upgraded charger.

- Typically are 100ah batteries, but higher ah models are available.

- Lithium batteries will enable installing an inverter to power 110-volt appliances from your 12-volt lithium batteries. See 110-volt power section below for more details.

Inboard lithium system charging options, from slowest to fastest:

- Solar panel array on vehicle or portable solar panels deployed

- Shore power at campground or residence

- Alternator charging while driving

Portable Lithium Solar Generators

Solar generators made by brands such as Jackery are a popular alternative to installing a full battery setup. These generators offer a simple, plug-and-work setup rather than requiring extensive effort to select, size, and install a 12-volt lithium-based electrical system.

Even with a battery system installed, I believe every vanlifer should carry a small solar generator, such as the small Jackery 240 I travel with. These units are excellent secondary power sources to recharge laptops, tablets, smartphones, etc. This keeps your primary system focused on coach lights, refrigerator, and other essentials. Even with a lithium-based electrical system, a small Jackery 240 is also a great, lightweight tool to use at a campsite outside the van.

Pros:

- All-in-one unit simplifies having lithium based power.

- No advanced skills are needed for a vanlifer to set up lithium power via one of these units.

- Portability means these units can be moved from the vehicle into a cabin or home base to power other needs, or supplement during a power failure.

- The cost of large solar generators, including sufficient solar portable panels for recharging, can be less than the cost to install an inboard lithium system.

Cons:

- Units large enough to provide the same level of power as inboard lithium batteries are heavy and bulky, thus require considerable storage space in the vehicle.

- Powering devices, including appliances, requires plugging into the solar generator wherever it sits, rather than using outlets wired in convenient places inside the vehicle.

- Solar generators have fewer recharging options than inboard systems, and may take longer to recharge. Relying on a large portable solar generator for significant power usage requires work to perfect a reasonably efficient recharging process to maintain power when needed.

- *There are not, as of this writing, large enough portable solar generators to power an A/C for as long as you would need to use it during a day.*

Portable solar generator charging options, from slowest to fastest:

- Unit power adapter via vehicle's 12-volt plug (only while driving)

- Portable solar panels deployed

- Shore power at campground or residence

Portable Solar Generator Summary

Portable solar generators can be a good solution if you accept their disadvantages. Long-term, I believe investing in an inboard lithium system is worthwhile, as it is more efficient, easier to use, and can be expanded as your budget allows.

110-volt Power Systems

While 12-volt power provides basic vanlife needs, there are good reasons to install equipment enabling 110-volt power options. These uses include running 110-volt appliances, faster battery recharging, and powering A/C. Providing 110-volt power for these situations usually occurs when plugged into shore power at a campground, or using a 110-volt plug at a residential house.

To run A/C or higher-wattage appliances without shore power would require a significant investment in lithium batteries and supporting equipment. In my van, I can run a variety of 110-volt appliances via my inverter powered by two lithium batteries, but to use my roof-top A/C, I have to use shore power.

This level of equipment requires more analysis of exact power needed, which is beyond the scope of this book. You can find a lot of resources via YouTube and Google to learn how others calculated their potential electricity loads. Typical components necessary to achieve off-grid 110-volt power, along with some tips and concerns include:

Alternator Charging

This option requires more advanced wiring to enable. By installing this, plus the appropriate battery charger, your coach batteries will recharge whenever you run your vehicles engine, whether driving or parked. This is the fastest method available to recharge batteries.

Automatic Transfer Switch

Device which intelligently senses which power is available (shore or inverter) then sends that power source to the outlet(s). Advanced experience is required to install an ATS, depending on the complexity of your electrical system.

Battery Charger

Chose a 110-volt model specific to your battery type. A charger can be a simple unit wired to your batteries and plugged into shore power with an appropriately sized extension cord. Or, you can hard-wire a 20- or 30-amp system designed to work when plugged into shore power via an external connector and a special, heavy-duty cable.

For 30-amp systems, use the RV-style external plug and cable since those have the correct plugs for using 30-amp service. Depending on equipment you plan to power from shore power, you can also set up a typical 20-amp system with a standard 110-volt plug. This option can also plug into shore power at campgrounds or parks, provided your site's power pedestal has 20-amp service.

Battery Monitor

Device which provides information about battery charge, condition, charge cycle count, and other vital information. Having a good battery monitor helps you avoid losing power, damage your batteries, decide when to use which type of recharging, and tracks your charge cycle counts so you know when to proactively replace your batteries.

Inverter

Device installed between your batteries and 110-volt outlets. Smaller inverters include one or two 110-volt outlets on their case. Installing an inverter is complicated, so DIYers who do not have electrical experience should consult a professional.

Inverters come in watt sizes, e.g., 2000 watt (2kw), 3000 watt (3kw), etc. The number indicates their peak load capabilities, but they also have a surge load rating (usually close to double). Surge load refers to the inverter's ability to handle the energy surge required when starting some appliances and motors. This is not energy you can use to run a more watt-intensive appliance.

A rule of thumb for how many lithium batteries you need with different size inverters: 1kw inverter works with one or more batteries, a 2kw needs two more batteries, and a 3kw needs three or more batteries.

When selecting an inverter, I recommend staying with recognized and trusted brands, e.g., Xantrex, Victron, Renogy, etc. Avoid the temptation of buying a cheaper, off-brand inverter whose reliability is unknown.

Sizing an inverter requires understanding the maximum number of devices which need power simultaneously, then adding up their wattage draws to determine which inverter size will work for you. Bigger is always better, of course, since you may add other appliances later. A rule of thumb for sizing is that the total wattage should be within 60-70% of the inverter's peak (NOT surge) load capacity. Thus, a total run wattage of approximately 1400 watts is appropriate for a 2000-watt inverter, and 2100 watts for a 3000 watt inverter. Essentially, choose the 2000-watt inverter if you will only be running basic appliances (such as a coffee maker, toaster, hot water kettle, rice maker, small laser printer, etc.), and you do not intend to run more than one or two at the same time.

If you want to run an air conditioner and induction stovetop as well, then you will need at least a 3000-watt inverter. Even then, those appliances should not be run at the same time. While both the A/C and induction stovetop can run via an inverter if you have enough lithium batteries installed, they will deplete a significant amount of your battery charge, making recharging for the next large power draw a challenge.

Note that powering your appliances through existing 110-volt outlets requires extensive work in the 110-volt fuse panel, and may require other wiring accessories. For simple appliance use, you can save time by wiring only one 110-volt outlet for inverter use, plus use the plugs on the inverter itself, if your inverter has them. To enable any 110-volt outlet to work from either the inverter or when plugged into shore power, you must also install an ATS (automatic transfer switch).

Lithium Batteries

Discussed above, these are currently the best option to power an off-grid 110-volt system, and significantly increase energy available to 12-volt items. The number of batteries you need depends on what devices you use in a given day. Two are best for most installs, but you may need four or more if you are a heavy power user, or wish to power an air conditioner, an induction cooktop, a microwave, or other high-wattage devices.

Miscellaneous Parts

Depending on which of the above components are in your system, there may be other smaller parts needed, e.g., bus bars, remote switches, extra fuse panels, sub fuse panels, etc. Working with a professional who has experience with vehicle battery electrical systems will help determine what you need.

Solar Charger

Device which controls the conversion of the solar panel's output to batteries as charging energy. If you are using lithium batteries, choose a charger optimized for these batteries. Typical chargers display how many amps or watts go to the batteries, which helps you position your panels for optimum solar energy capture. Experience will show you how many amps you need to pull in during sunlight to recharge the energy lost through the evening and overnight.

Solar Panels

Unless you plan to always stay at parks and campgrounds with shore power, you will benefit from traveling with a solar panel solution regardless of battery type. Whether you install an array of solar panels on the roof or travel with a suitcase solar panel, using solar energy makes vanlife easier and better.

The size and number of solar panels you need depends on how many batteries you install, the frequency of the load on the batteries, and space on your roof or elsewhere on your vehicle. As a reference, I have two solar panels on my van's roof which total 260 watts, plus I travel with a Jackery 100-watt folding panel. That combination keeps my two lithium batteries charged up in all seasons, although I do not travel much in winter where there is snow, which is a challenge for solar recharging.

Suitcase panels typically plug into the charging system via an installed external solar port. You can set these portable units up at the right angle to the available sunlight and move them over the day to keep up with the sun's movement. This helps in conditions like southern winter camping, when the sun's angle is low in the sky. In such conditions, any flat solar panels on the roof will not receive much solar energy unless you build in a tilting mechanism. In my experience over the winter in Southwest Arizona, my 100-watt suitcase panel pulled in roughly 70% of the amps going to my batteries, despite only being 28% of the total capacity of my solar array (two roof panels and the portable panel).

FUEL: GAS, DIESEL, PROPANE

Of the various vanlife resources, fuel to run your engine and propane devices may be the easiest to get on the road. Excluding a national crisis, gas or diesel for your engine is readily available, with a few exceptions in remote areas. For propane, most cities and towns have multiple sources for refilling, since it is also a common household fuel in rural areas and for home grills.

Tips and guidance:

Gas or diesel:

- There is not much difference between using gas or diesel in vanlife versus in a personal vehicle. Since it powers your vehicle's mobility, and you may travel in more remote places, it is important to pay attention to your fuel gauge and know approximately how many miles you have left in the tank.

- There are smartphone apps to help you find the best-priced gas or diesel, or Google Maps can be used to find fuel stops along your route. My own travel approach is to stop and fill up when at a quarter tank, plus fill up regardless of fuel level when driving into a remote area to stay several days or longer.

Propane:

- Good sources to look for are businesses like Tractor Supply, U-Haul, local propane dealers, and sometimes gas stations/convenience stores. As with gas or diesel, apps and Google Maps help in finding propane filling locations. **Never attempt to fill propane yourself**, since it is a dangerous gas if improperly used, and tanks become unsafe if improperly filled.

- Another challenge with propane is knowing how much propane remains in your tank, combined with a sense of how much you use for heating or cooking. Some RVs come with installed propane gauges, although the one in my Travato was not accurate enough to be helpful.

- If you are using small, disposable propane tanks, carry a spare. If you have an underneath or enclosed propane bottle or tank, see "Appendix B – Resources & Links" for a recommendation of a Bluetooth propane monitor I use on my van's six-gallon propane tank.

WASTE & DUMPING

While not the most pleasant of tasks, the reality of vanlife is that you will need to figure out how to safely handle human liquid and solid waste. If more than one person is traveling, this can be bigger challenge if the desire is to provide a fully onboard system for both types of waste.

Going #1 & #2

See "Chapter 7: Personal Stuff – Challenges & Solutions, Toileting" for options and details.

Other tips:

- When available, use public facilities while traveling.

- When camping at parks or campgrounds, use their toilets.

- When boondocking in the wild, and there is no facility nearby or you have no solution with you, the old-school backpacker method of carrying a shovel, walking 20′ off a trail, digging a hole 8″ or deeper, doing your business, and filling the hole back in with dirt. This is still an acceptable option in many wilderness areas, *so long as you do it correctly.*

Waste Removal

You will need to find a designated dump station to safely empty your waste if you have an onboard waste system, or even if you are using liquid waste bottles.

- *If using the poo-in-a-bag approach,* then find a dumpster to dispose of the bag.

- *If using a dump station,* you will usually pay a fee. Fee-based campgrounds or parks usually have a dump station on-site included as part of your camping fee. Sometimes small municipalities have free public dump stations at their water- and waste-disposal facilities. You can find these locations using apps (see "Appendix B – Resources & Links").

WATER

In vanlife, the water you carry onboard serves many purposes: body waste systems, cooking, dishwashing, drinking, hand-washing, hair-washing, rinsing feet and muddy shoes, showering, teeth-brushing, and probably more. For practicality, vanlifers should consider carrying only safe-for-drinking water for all purposes. It is complicated to carry both drinkable water and non-potable water and easy to mix up the two, with potentially dire results.

I travel with a 20-gallon on-board fresh water tank that I fill with safe-to-drink water, but only use for showering, washing dishes, etc. I carry a second, more filtered, three-gallon water jug for brushing teeth, drinking, and cooking. Many vanlifers will drink out of the onboard fresh water tank, but I prefer the taste and the peace of mind of using this extra jug for ingestible water. If I cannot find a filtered water station to refill my three-gallon jug, I would not worry about temporarily using water from my 20-gallon tank.

If you find yourself consistently unable to get enough safe-to-drink water, you might consider two water storage solutions: one for ingestible water, the other for cleaning, showering, etc. I would be reluctant, however, to use non-potable water to shower with, because our skin is essentially our body's largest organ and whatever is in the water will likely get through the skin. RVers usually use non-potable water only for flushing out their black waste tanks at dump stations, filling radiators, etc.

Finding Safe-to-Drink Water

As you travel, finding fresh water can be unpredictable. Being aware of how much water you have left will give you time to find a refill source before you run out.

- In some areas of the U.S., such as the southwest, drinking water kiosks are easy to find. These convenient locations let you fill five gallons for ~$1, or ~$.25 per gallon. This source works great for refillable containers. For those who have large, installed fresh water tanks, these kiosks sometime have extra hoses and systems to accommodate larger-volume water fills.

- Most good-sized grocery stores have filtered water machines to fill one- to five-gallon jugs inexpensively. This is a better option than buying bottled water off their shelves and wasting plastic containers.

- Typically, those with installed tanks prefer to find a hose bib for water refilling. These can usually be found at state and RV parks, some federal forest campgrounds, trucks stops, some municipal parks, or other public places. Be cautious to only fill from those with clean, okay smelling water, and via a pipe system. And be sure to filter the incoming water and use a RV water pressure regulator to control the water pressure going into your system to avoid damage to hoses and fittings.

- Only use specified, drinking-water-safe hoses to fill your tanks from any source. *Never* **use a regular garden hose since it has harmful chemicals in the hose and connections that make water run through them unsuitable for ingestion.**

- There may be times you have no choice but to fill up with whatever water you can find. In these cases, if you filter this water as described in the next bullet, it will probably be okay.

- Unless your water source is from a kiosk or store, it is a good idea to filter or double-filter any water you use for drinking or cooking. Vanlifers typically use the readily-available, blue tube water filter on their hose before the water enters into containers or their onboard tank. Some vanlifers then filter the water from the onboard tank a second time through a high-quality filter that gets rid of most bacteria and metals. This can be at the faucet if you have an installed system, or via a popular pitcher, such as a Pur model with an advanced filter. See the links above for the RV water filter and water pressure regulator.

Storage Options

Ask a dozen vanlifers how they carry water and you will hear different clever and not-so-clever solutions. How you choose depends on your rig, how much you need, your safety tolerance, and where you will store the containers.

- *Basic* – Any drinking-water safe container (hopefully BPA-free) suffices for storing water, depending on storage space, water use, and how many jugs you want to deal with each time you refill water. Over time, it is probably a good idea to recycle these containers and get new ones.

- *Condensed* – Purchase one or two new, empty, BPA-free, three- or five-gallon water jugs with the wide-mouth tops. Commonly used in office water dispensers, you can find them at most Walmarts, etc. With one of these, you can insert a USB-rechargeable pump on the top and dispense water easily without a mess.

- *Installed* – Purchase a RV-ready, fresh water tank to install in a cabinet, then install a valve to empty it, and a hose connection to fill up. If possible, also install a gravity fill so you can pour water in if pressurized water is unavailable. Add a basic cabinet, a sink and faucet with a manual in-faucet pump or wire, and install an electric pump to bring water through the faucet. Optionally, you can install the secondary water filter in the line leading to this faucet. Most manufactured and custom-built RVs use this tank/sink/faucet approach.

Waste Water

Using water inside your vehicle requires a storage solution for the waste or excess water, and a process to empty it.

- *Basic* – Work over a large bucket when using water (e.g., a three- or five-gallon plastic bucket commonly found at a home improvement store). This can double as part of a simple shower or toilet. Can be messy, but it is one simple solution.

- *Better* – Build a small cabinet and inset a large, stainless steel mixing bowl into the counter as a sink. You can remove it to empty it, or drill a hole in the bottom and install a simple drain using plumber's caulk and a short, drop pipe into a portable container below. Check the waste storage frequently to avoid overspill, then manually empty. Water supply for this approach can be from a gallon jug or a larger jug connected by tube to a hand-pump/12-volt pump faucet.

- *Best* – Install a sink as above, then install a grey water tank in a cabinet. Connect the sink drain through a p-trap to the grey tanks. You will need to install a valved connection at the lowest point to drain the tank, which could be via a simple garden hose-type connector, or a RV-type dump connection with a typical RV dump hose. Note that in most U.S. states, you must dump grey water tanks into a dump station and not onto the open ground. The size of the grey tank depends on your space, but should be 10-gallon at minimum, or 20 gallons ideally.

CHAPTER 11
SO WHAT ABOUT PLACES TO STAY?

> Oh the places you'll go.
>
> DR. SEUSS

Now you have your vehicle picked out, set up, and ready to roll, *where can you go?*

What are your options for where to stay overnight, a few days, a few weeks, or maybe a month or more in one place?

There are a lot of options, some plentiful, others scarce, depending on which part of the U.S. you travel through.

BOONDOCKING

This method is one of the more popular Vanlife options, especially if you are traveling in a van or small RV (Class B, or perhaps a C). Boondocking, simply defined, is staying on undeveloped (or lightly developed) open land and relying on resources you carry in your vehicle for your needs. Boondocking typically has no hookups of electric or sewer, no bathrooms or pit toilets, and no showers or trash receptacles. What it does have, and usually in abundance, is nature, space, and acres of privacy.

You can also boondock in the driveway of a friend, at a rest area, in a Walmart parking lot, etc. Another similar term is wildcamping, which is essentially boondocking in more remote natural areas. For our purposes, we will focus on self-sustained camping in your vehicle on natural land, regardless of the land's ownership.

Pros:

- *Closer to nature* – Typically most boondocking spots are within forests or designated wilderness areas.

- *Privacy* – Boondocking typically (but not always) provides a good amount of space between you and the next boondocker, often without seeing anyone else camping around you.

- *Price* – Usually, boondocking locations are free. BLM land requires a 14-day permit, but usually no fee, since there is no organized campground or only minimal services (often none).

- *Shower* – You can set up a solar shower outside your vehicle to use when needed.

Cons:

- *Resources* – Typically, boondocking means relying on your own resources: water, propane, fuel, food, and charged batteries. There is no dump site for your grey or black tank wastes, nor trash facilities. Be sure to plan to take any trash with you when you go, and do not leave it, bury it, or burn it in the wild.

- *Isolation* – Can be a pro, but for some, this may be a negative since being alone means isolation and being on your own should you need help. Those who travel and have concerns for safety may need to be selective where they boondock.

- *Cell service* – Boondocking may mean poor or no cell connection.

Tips, tricks, & techniques:

- Be sure to stock up on resources and dump your tanks before boondocking if you plan to be out for more than a few days. Once you have experience boondocking and managing your resources, you can estimate more accurately how long you can boondock before needing to replenish resources.

- Stick to camping in places that appear to be campsites, i.e., do not drive on wild vegetation to make a camp. Most boondocking areas have spots used as campsites before, and you should choose one of these.

- Be alert for that inner voice that may warn you to not camp at a spot. There are always other site opportunities.

- Do not take your vehicle down dirt roads or off in the wild terrain if you are not equipped or set up for such travel (e.g., four-wheel drive, high clearance, carrying recovery equipment such as tow strap, recovery boards, shovel).

- Move to another spot if others arrive and camp nearby, making you feel uneasy.

- Pay attention to the forecasted weather for the general location, particularly high wind or thunderstorm warnings.

- Despite the obvious allure of camping next to a stream or lake, be aware of terrain features and signs of previous flooding. This awareness, combined with being weather-aware, can help avoid high-water problems.

- Equip your vehicle with a good cell booster if cellular connectivity is important to while boondocking. If connectivity is critical, as for those who work in their vehicles, then consider a satellite backup system, and/or traveling with two cell networks/devices.

- Carry a small, portable solar charger, such as the Jackery 240 (with a companion portable solar panel) I travel with. Use this to recharge your phone and computers, and keep that energy draw off your coach batteries while boondocking.

- Equip your vehicle with an external solar panel connector and consider traveling with a portable solar panel. If you need to park your vehicle in the shade, your rooftop solar panels will not recharge well, but you could set out a portable solar panel to help recharging.

MEMBERSHIP, NATIONAL, STATE, & RV PARKS

These locations offer organized, *fee*-based campsites in a managed park. Vanlifers who crave social interaction may be happier staying at these parks, where socialization is easier. For these options, advanced reservations in high season may be necessary to get a campsite, although some RVers do luck out and grab recently cancelled campsites.

Differences:

- *Membership parks* – Privately owned, these staffed parks typically have an annual fee (besides a one-time registration fee), plus a reduced campsite fee. Some have add-on fees for extras, such as electricity, dump station, etc. Membership typically has some usage limitations, such as only allowing a certain number of days or weeks you can stay at that membership's parks around the country. These memberships can be expensive, but many travelers in larger rigs (e.g., Class A and large trailers) enjoy the parks because they guarantee a campsite, plus offer full amenities. Parks range from Thousand Trails at the high end, to more club-like memberships, which offer access to a limited number of RV parks around the country, to simple membership systems, which provide discounts at participating parks, e.g., Escapees, Passport America, Good Sam.

- *National parks* – Owned by the U.S. National Park System and staffed with rangers, workers, and volunteers, these campgrounds can be excellent or bare bones, depending on the park. Amenities and resources vary. Note that more national parks are now restricting overnight access to RVs over a certain length. If you drive a Class A or tow a long RV trailer, be sure to verify what the park allows. Note that the U.S. America the Beautiful or Senior Pass can waive entrance fees and often a discount on campsites.

- *State parks* – Owned by each state and managed through a state parks department. Typically staffed with rangers, workers, and volunteers. Varies greatly in quality, cleanliness, and amenities by state and often within each state. Usually a good value for the campsite fee, but can depend on what amenities and resources each has available. Residents of the state can, for an annual fee, buy a pass that waives the park visit fee and sometimes provides a campground discount.

- *RV parks* – Privately owned and usually on-site managed, these parks typically offer more socialization opportunities and services than other park options, sometimes even gift shops and restaurants. They are generally pricey to stay at, but if the benefits are what you are looking for, RV parks exist all over the country. so finding one is easy. Finding one with available campsites, however, is not always easy!

Organized park pros and cons:

Pros:

- *Resources* – Typically, organized parks have resources such as water, shore power, dump station, toilets or pit toilets, trash, and sometimes showers and laundry facilities. Most membership and RV parks have all of those, but state parks and national parks may only have some of those resources provided.

- *Guaranteed stays* – These organized parks typically require reservations. At some locations you may be able to get a campsite if the park has a recent cancellation. Additionally, many state and national parks keep some campsites available for first-come, first-serve (FF).

- *Socialization* – If you like to socialize with other RVers and vanlife travelers, organized parks offer good opportunities for interaction.

- *Special nature proximity* – Staying in national parks and state parks may get you closer to amazing natural wonders, sometimes within walking or hiking distance. I stayed one night at Devil's Tower National Monument and was able to get a campsite where the tower filled my van's sliding door view. I had an awesome time just sitting and staring at that majestic, unique geographic wonder.

Cons:

- *Planning* – Most of the time you need to plan ahead to reserve a site. In-season reservations are difficult to get, sometimes requiring reserving a year or so ahead, e.g., Florida state park reservations during January-March, or the big National Parks out west during the prime summer season.

- *Expense* – Park fees can range from $15 to $150 per day, depending on what your vehicle is and where the park is. Membership parks have a different fee arrangement since you join for an annual fee, plus a reduced day-use fee.

- *Crowds* – Campsites in a typical park are close together, and even closer in a typical RV park.

Tips, tricks, & techniques:

- Some organized parks are better and more honest in each campsite's description of things that may be critical to you, such as: whether the park is sun or shaded (is solar recharging critical for you?), how level the site is (matters less if your rig has levelers, more in a van that needs blocks or rocks to level), what size rig or vehicle will fit, and whether the site is a back-in or pull-through layout. Be sure to check for those requirements, or call and ask questions if any are critical to your vehicle's capabilities.

- Many reservation systems offer photographs of each site, which can be helpful or misleading. Rely on specific listed details more than photos, campsite map, and Google Maps satellite view of a park's terrain.

- Read the cancellation policy before reserving. Some are fair, some quite onerous.

FEDERAL CAMPGROUNDS

Federally owned campgrounds are another option for an organized park that provides some fee-based amenities. These can be part of the National Forest System, the Army Corps of Engineers campgrounds, many designated Recreation Areas, and others. Most have a reservation system, are inexpensive compared to other organized parks, and provide basic services. These locations are my preferred locations for fee-based campsites, and they usually give a discount for federal pass program holders (America the Beautiful, Seniors Pass, others). See "Appendix B – Resources & Links" for websites.

EXTENDED STAYS

Most of the options above limit your stay to no more than 14 days in a row. If you want to stay in one place longer, then you will need to choose a different extended stay option.

- *BLM land* – Stays are limited to 14 days, but you can move to another BLM more than 25 miles away and stay another 14 days. Also, after leaving a specific BLM area, you can return and stay another 14 days if 28 days have passed since you last stayed there. There are full-time vanlifers who migrate from warmer, Southern Arizona BLM land in the winter up to cooler, Northern Arizona BLM land in the summer, moving strategically every 14 days to stay within the BLM rules.

- *BLM / LTVA* – There are seven BLM locations in Southeast California and Southwest Arizona designated as Long-Term Visitor Areas, where you can buy an $80 permit to stay 30 days, or pay $180 for the full, designated winter season from September 15 to April 15. LTVAs vary on amenities, ranging from trash service only to more compete services such as trash, water, dump station, pit toilets, and showers. These LTVAs were created to meet the needs and demands of the retirees (affectionately known as snow birds) who escape winter in the north to these warmer LTVA locations.

- *BLM / Recreation Areas* – Fee-based, 14-day stays allowed, or you may purchase an annual pass to save and stay at a specific BLM recreation area. Amenities vary, but usually only trash and pit toilets.

ON-THE-WAY OVERNIGHT STAYS

Sometimes you need a safe place to pull over and sleep while en route during a multi-day trip. You need a convenient place on your route that requires no setup or cost to stay overnight. Sadly, some of these options are gone, thanks to careless and selfish RVers and vanlifers. Their bad behavior, such as trashing parking lots, camping out with BBQ grills and lawn furniture, or staying until kicked out, ruined it for the rest of us well-behaved travelers. Fortunately, there are still many options available.

Big-box Retail

Up until a few years ago, you could stop at almost any Walmart, Cabelas, Sam's Club, CostCo, etc., and stay a night. As mentioned, abuse of these locations, plus a growing number of ordinances created partly out of fear of homeless people living in parked vehicles, removed many Walmarts and Cabela's from this list. You can still use Walmarts if posted signs allow, and sometimes *despite* the signs, if you drive an inconspicuous vehicle (car, mini-van, cargo van, small Class B, etc.). Other spots such as CostCo allow overnighting, although this varies by location, requiring you to call or ask the store manager if you can stay overnight. Being a member of Costco or Sam's Club does not automatically allow you to stay there; if they allow overnighting, anyone can stay.

Restaurants

Cracker Barrel is a favorite location for many RVers/vanlifers to overnight at, and I have never found one that did not allow it. Most have signage in the back parking lot marked for RV parking. When I stay there, I usually park in the back first, then move to the front after the restaurant closes. I find it quieter to park in the front and avoid occasional impolite RVers who run their generators throughout the night.

Cracker Barrels are convenient, located in most good-sized towns or larger, near interstates, but usually noisy (interstate traffic and the dumpster service shows up at 4 or 5 in the morning). They are undeniably a tasty place to have dinner before sleeping, or a great breakfast before departing!

Boondockers Welcome/Harvest Host

This is an annual fee-based club, but joining allows you to stay at a host's house, business, farm, golf course, etc. for free. Harvest Hosts locations, such as the farms, wineries, cheese makers, etc. have an expectation that you will buy some of their goods in exchange for staying.

The Boondockers Welcome section (acquired in 2021 by Harvest Hosts) are private residences or businesses which allow overnighting for at least one or two days, but often up to five days. These hosts are RV owners/travelers and enjoy meeting others who love to travel. There is no reciprocation required nor cost to stay, although some may charge a modest fee for electric hookup, etc.

Once a member, you can use the online site or an app to search and request reservations at a host's location. The Boondockers Welcome private residences are often great places to stay a few days versus Walmart or a rest area. I recently stayed at one in Albuquerque, New Mexico, which is a place notoriously difficult to boondock, or even stealth camp. Having a Boondockers Welcome host there allowed me to stay for several days to explore the area, rather than at a campsite an hour away.

Community Parks

Some small towns and cities allow overnighting at their parks or facilities such as recreation areas or municipal services for waste and water management. If a city has a fairground, these are sometimes available to overnight at for free or a modest fee.

Hospitals

A busy hospital has a lot of vehicles coming and going around the clock, plus it is not uncommon for a patients' family members to stay overnight in their parking lot. Varies by hospital, but can be a good option.

Industrial Neighborhoods

Almost all mid-size towns or larger have these areas, and they frequently have commercial trucks and vans parked along their streets. It is easy to blend in and stay overnight, provided you keep a low profile. Avoid any dead-end roads, and try to stay somewhat central inside the industrial area, avoiding the perimeter. If the area you are eyeing is run-down and the parked vehicles look beat up, move on to somewhere else.

Multi-family Residential Areas

While stealth camping curbside in a single-family residence area is asking for a knock on the door in the middle of the night, you will usually be okay parking in front of large multi-family developments, especially in larger cities. These typically have a lot of vehicles parked curbside in front of them that are easy to blend in with, as with industrial areas.

Rest Areas

Mention sleeping at a rest area, and a friend or relative may tell you it is dangerous. This is not true when there are other cars and vans around. Ever notice how many big trucks park overnight at rest areas? Tons. While there is no guarantee every rest area in every U.S. state allows overnight parking, many do. Watch for signs, but park in a spot appropriate to your rig. Truckers, unlike you, are required by law to stop and sleep and they need those long spaces at rest areas. Do not be a jerk and take one of their spots away from them. They have fewer options than you do where they can safely stop and sleep.

Truck Service Areas

Another option, although noisy, are truck stops such as Flying J, Love's, Pilot, etc. Most allow overnight parking. Remember though, these facilities are for truckers who must by law stop and sleep within time restrictions, and who have fewer places than you to choose from. If you stay here, park well away from the area where they park.

Tips, tricks, & techniques:

- In today's vanlife world, the #1 thing to look for is signage specifically prohibiting overnighting in any of these locations. There are some exceptions, but if a sign states *"No overnight parking (or camping),"* then move on to something else. Sometimes it is a city ordinance (perhaps even recently enacted due to the bad players ruining it for the rest of us) or a new policy of the facility owner.

- If there is an abundance of "no overnight" signs and yet there are a lot of run-down (and probably not running) RVs, vans, or campers parked there, move on: it is likely a spot where the local police look the other way only for these homeless residents in vehicles, plus your neighbors may be troublesome to a new, shiny vehicle overnighting with them.

- When in doubt and at a retail store or restaurant, call or ask the manager for permission.

- If you are parking curbside, generally move on if there are no other vehicles parked there.

- Always leave early, wherever you overnight. This avoids interfering with a business's customers or employees, and reduces being noticed by residents or locals.

- If you need to stay more than one night in an area where you are stealth camping, move to a different spot each night. A patrol car noticing you in a spot one night will probably not check you out, but if they see you there on consecutive nights, you will probably get a knock on the door.

- Be respectful. If you stealth camp, or stop at a place not designated as a campground, do not feel entitled to set up camp, put out the RV mat, the lawn chairs, etc. Stay within your vehicle and be low-key.

- Cover your windows, slide the privacy curtain (if you have one) that separates the coach part of your van from the cab seats if you have one, and be unobtrusive.

- As mentioned, but needs reinforcing: if you overnight at a place designated for interstate truckers, do not use their spaces. Truckers are not happy when you pull your Class A RV, or your pickup truck towing a long RV trailer into one of their spots. Many drivers do it, but it is bad form in my opinion, and most truckers agree.

- Plan to do whatever you need to do outside your vehicle before you settle in at your stealth camping spot. Do not work on the outside of your rig in a Walmart parking lot, or when curb-parked in a small town. This will draw attention and passerby may think you are living in the van, thus increasing the odds of someone checking on you.

SUMMARY

Be smart, be wise, and listen to your common sense when choosing to stay in any unmanaged or unsupervised location. There are ample places to stay, both paid and free, but some take a little extra time and effort to find. For more specifics on how to find some of these listed above, see "Appendix B – Resources & Links."

CHAPTER 12
THOSE PESKY
RULES & REQUIREMENTS

To know the rules of the game, you have to be educated.

LL COOL J

Everything covered so far focuses on choices in vanlife: which vehicle, where to stay, how to travel, etc. This section covers the required legal and financial stuff necessary in vanlife.

FULL-TIME VANLIFERS

If your vehicle will be your legal home (i.e., you have no physical residence you can use as a legal residence), there are several issues and processes applicable to you and your vehicle.

PLEASE NOTE: You need to meet ALL the requirements your former state has for NOT being a resident to avoid that state claiming you are still a resident who owes state income taxes on your earnings for that year. All states have a checklist of what defines residency, so be sure to review your current state's residency rules and understand them. It is not always just an address, but timing/length of residency, whether you worked there, and other issues.

For your new state, you will need to file paperwork and meet qualifications to establish a legal domicile residency. This process will enable you to acquire the various items listed in the following sections.

Driver's License

If you are full-timing, you will need to get a new driver's license in the state you choose as your new legal residency or domicile. Each state has different requirements and processes for a new resident driver's license, including different gap periods before you are required to get a new license.

Financial Institutions

Banks and securities are institutions that usually *do not* accept your new domicile residency address and require a true, physical address on record. For this, you can usually use a relative's home address. This option will mean mail from these institutions will go to your relative's home, so arrangements may be necessary to have their communications forwarded to you.

When you file your federal or state income tax forms use the address you used to establish your residency or legal domicile (often the same as the mail-forwarding service address if you used that option).

Healthcare Insurances

As a full-time vanlifer, you will need to confirm your healthcare policies will work under your new residency and where you travel. Some insurance, such as Medicare-related options, may provide coverage only within your residency state. Changing states may require updating these policies or switching to different providers to ensure you have healthcare, emergency procedures, and prescription drug coverage wherever you travel.

Mail-forwarding Service

Unless you use a friend or relative's address as your residency, you must set up a legal address through a mail-forwarding service. The mail-forwarding service is how you will get a legal address that the state accepts for everything from a new driver's license to registering and titling your vehicle, license plates, insurance, and more.

See "Appendix B – Resources & Links" for several popular mail-forwarding services. Each have similar features, such as mail scanning (receive scans of incoming mail via PDF), mail shredding (for junk mail, or after viewing mail through the scanning feature), and mail forwarding to an address of your choice. Your choice affects which state you chose for your new residency, which will affect vehicle insurance cost, where you vote absentee from, the process required for setting up a domicile, and whether you have to return to that state periodically or not.

Note that using this address for receiving magazines or packages is not a good idea since the cost of forwarding these to you is prohibitive, whereas forwarding first-class mail is affordable.

When you set up an account with one of these services, consider changing your bills and other frequent mail items to paperless options, received electronically. This will result in less mail at your forwarder, less mail to scan and read, and less to forward to you, thus potentially lower cost for the service.

Registration & Title

The registration and titling process for your vanlife vehicle is almost the same as when buying a personal-use car. The one difference is that some state register and title RVs or camper vans with wet showers as a motorhome. How each state classifies a vehicle as a motorhome varies, so check your state guidelines to be sure. This designation usually costs more, and in some states it comes with a special license plate. Be aware that some co-op, homeowner, or zoning restrictions prohibit parking of motorhomes or RVs.

Residency

You can set up residency in any state, but the majority have requirements (proof of residence, utility bill, time in residence, etc.) that full-time vanlifers cannot meet. There are three states most full-time RVers and vanlifers use for legal residency without actually living there.

Which of these three you choose depends on your situation, general travel plans, healthcare insurance coverage, and which process and annual renewal options you are most comfortable with. Regardless which state you pick, you will still need a true, physical address to use for financial matters (see above). Also note that all three require in-state, in-person driver license application and granting. See "Appendix B – Resources & Links" for links with more details.

Florida

Pros:

- No personal income tax
- No vehicle state inspections
- Can renew driver's license online
- Great options for Medicare-aged people
- Lower vehicle registration fees
- Resident discounts for state park campsites and other places
- Popular and reliable mail forwarder in St. Augustine

Cons:

- Higher vehicle insurance
- Jury duty exemption can be harder to get (although I got an out-of-state traveling exemption the year I was a full-time Florida domicile resident)
- VIN verification by law enforcement for initial registration (can use a verification letter from another state's DMV)

South Dakota

Pros:

- No personal state income tax
- Low vehicle excise tax
- Easy jury exemption
- No vehicle state inspections
- Lower insurance costs

Cons:

- Vehicle registration can be more costly
- Must stay one night in-state, with receipt, when getting driver's license (in person)
- Must return to renew driver's license after five years (after that, can renew online)
- Timing is critical for setting up, unless you do so in the summer, since South Dakota has brutally cold winters

Texas

Pros:

- No personal income tax
- Driver's license renewable once online
- Flat annual vehicle inspection cost
- Medium-price vehicle insurance
- Popular and reliable Escapees mail-forward service, which some claim helps with jury duty exemptions

Cons:

- Requires in-state annual vehicle inspection
- RVs over a specific weight require an exam to get a special driver's license
- Jury duty exposure

Vehicle Insurance Add-ons

When you live in your vehicle full-time, you have similar financial and legal exposures as you did when living in your house or apartment, e.g., liability for anyone on your property, or coverage for your household possessions and full-time use of that home or apartment.

If you live full-time in your vehicle, you will need to add coverage for these house-similar options. Depending on your vehicle type, most insurance companies have an option for full-time living coverage for these extra liabilities, and to cover personal possessions inside the vehicle. Not disclosing you are living in the vehicle full-time could, under certain circumstances, deny your insurance claim for an accident, theft, etc.

Special Concern for DIY Vanlifers:

Most insurance companies **will not insure** the materials and equipment you install in your van or vehicle if you do the work. When you purchase a converted van or RV from a manufacturer, then insurance covers all the equipment installed.

While you cannot cover most of your DIY materials and build, you can add a rider (at extra cost) to list some equipment (e.g., lithium batteries, inverter, solar panels) as personal equipment and thus provide some coverage for those items. But you cannot cover your own labor or that of outsourced installers on any DIY equipment installed.

Voting

As of this writing, all three of the noted domicile residency states allow you to register to vote based on the address you use as your domicile.

PART-TIME VANLIFERS

As a part-time traveler, life is simpler than a full-timer. There are a few differences depending on your situation and and how much you will travel in your vehicle.

Insurance

As with registration, insuring a RV or camper van is similar to insuring a passenger car, with one difference: your insurer will ask how many days per year you will spend in the RV/camper van (and how many miles you will drive, typically). This disclosure affects your insurance rate somewhat, but as with full-time vanlifers, failing to be reasonably accurate with this detail could cause a claim denial.

Registration & Title

See "Registration & Title" section in the "Full-time Vanlifers" section above.

DISCOVERY

I wander to know,
and travel to learn,
hoping nature will show
all that I yearn.

My path may be long,
and challenges true,
but desire's strong,
to see things through.

I won't know where,
until each day's taste,
I go without care,
and without haste.

Naysayers mean well,
yet my purpose is clear,
to write stories that tell
of wandering past fear.

APPENDIX A - VANLIFE TERMINOLOGY

AGM – Acronym for sealed (a)bsorbant (g)lass (m)at lead-acid batteries, which are designed to provide power for RVs and camper vans. This battery type needs monitoring to ensure voltage stays above 12.1, or calcification can occur, which results in a reduced ability to hold a charge. Currently AGMS are standard batteries in most RVs and camper vans, but lithium batteries are appearing more often as their technology advances and costs decrease.

Black tank – Sewage tank to collect waste from an onboard toilet. Industry-standard waste gate with a connector for a waste hose allows emptying the tank at a designated dump site. If using both black and grey tanks, then the waste gate may include two levers, one for each tank to release its contents. Usually has level sensors and a read-out panel indicating when tank is full.

BLM – Bureau of Land Management. U.S. department agency managing over 245 million acres of land, mostly in the western U.S. Much of this land is available for boondocking, and some locations have organized campgrounds. Where BLM camping exists, it is free, but with limits on how long you can stay.

Boondocking, boondock – Camping in a vehicle on open land without supporting resources such as electricity, fresh water, dump station, trash, picnic tables or grilling/fire pits. Also called dispersed camping or wild camping.

Boosters (cellular or Wi-Fi) – Electronic devices for amplifying cellular or Wi-Fi signals. Note when no signal is available, a booster will not help; they can only amplify or improve the signal if one exists.

Cab – In a van, the area in front with a driver and passenger seat; term used to separate the zones: cab in front, coach in the rest of the van.

Campground – Organized and managed area set aside for tent and vehicle camping. Usually has developed camp sites, often with connections (water, electricity, or sanitary waste), picnic tables, and grilling/fire pits. Some campgrounds have showers and public restrooms or pit toilets. Campgrounds are typically fee-based and usually staffed. Some campgrounds may have volunteer camp hosts who stay at the campground in their RV or trailer.

Car camping – Using a passenger vehicle to camp typically means sleeping inside the vehicle rather than in an outside tent. There are many variations of car camping, but this generally means a temporary setup for camping out of the vehicle, and later emptying the vehicle to use as a traditional passenger car.

Cassette toilet – Unit with an integrated, removable waste tank carried separately to empty at a dump station, rest area toilet, pit toilet, or home/gas station toilet. Becoming more prevalent in camper vans and Class B RVs due to minimal space required. Cassette toilets typically have waste tanks of three-to-five gallons, compared to black tanks, which typically hold 20 gallons or more.

Chassis battery – Battery (usually automotive-grade lead-acid type) used to start your vehicle and run its accessories.

Coach – The zone behind the cab in a van (or any vehicle designating the living area from the driving area).

Coach battery – Battery providing 12-volt power to your coach or the RV or camper van buildout. Typically one or more AGM batteries, or preferably a lithium battery system.

Digital nomad – Traveling worker, roaming from place to place using mobile connectivity while working for others or managing their own online business. Digital nomads typically have advanced connectivity devices and systems, and often travel with more than one cellular network to ensure connecting to the internet as needed.

Dispersed camping – see Boondocking.

Dumping – Emptying a vehicle's waste tanks into an established dump site. Most organized campgrounds, some BLM properties, or small city or town waste facilities, etc., have suitable dump facilities. Many charge a dump fee, unless you pay to camp at the facility.

Fresh water tank – Closed tank holding potable water. Typically has a hose-fitting for filling from an external potable water source, and/or a gravity fill to fill from bottles or filtered water kiosks. If the fresh water tank is new, you should sanitize before first use and again at least annually to control contamination. It is recommended to use a water filter before the water enters the tank, and again at the sink, if you are using the fresh tank water for drinking or cooking. Some vanlifers with fresh water tanks also carry three- to five-gallon jugs of filtered water for drinking and cooking, and use the fresh water tank only for dish cleaning, hand washing, showering, etc. DIY vanlifers often create a fresh water supply system consisting of a variety of refillable plastic bottles or jugs versus an installed tank, pump, and plumbing line system.

Gas/diesel heater – Advanced heating system run by the vehicle's fuel. Considered the best dry heat source available for a van, but is an expensive option. Typically with a built-in shutoff if the fuel source drops to one fourth of the tank to avoid being stranded.

Glamping – Coined term from "glamorous camping" for a vanlife ultra style: the best of everything, no compromises, and mimicking affluent living.

GPS trackers – Handheld device used by hikers and overlanders to track their GPS position at all times without relying on cellular signals. Units have a HELP button to use for emergencies or rescue if the user becomes injured and unable to hike out or travel.

Grey tank – Tank for holding waste water from sinks and sometimes showers. Industry-standard waste gate with a connector for a waste hose allows emptying at a dump site. If both black/grey tanks installed, waste gate may include two levers, one for each tank to release its contents. Tank usually has level sensors and read-out panels to indicate when tank is full. Note most U.S. states consider dumping grey tanks no different than black tanks, and thus require using a designated dump site. Only a few states remain which allow on-ground grey tank dumping. DIY vanlifers sometimes rig a simple grey tank system via a large jug placed under a sink in a cabinet, then manually dump the grey water jug when full.

High top – Refers to an option on vans which extends the interior ceiling height on vans/RV Class Bs to allow standing up inside.

Lithium – Battery type prized for its deep charge usage without damaging the battery, unlike AGM batteries. If installed under a vehicle, must be self-heating or enclosed in a heat-controlled box. Lithium batteries will not recharge at a certain low temperature point until they warm up above that threshold, although they can still provide power.

LTVA – Long-term visitor area designation of BLM land in the southwestern U.S. RVers, vanlifers, and car campers can obtain a 30-day or a 7-month seasonal pass to stay at any BLM LTVA campground. LTVAs vary in amenities provided. As an example, the Imperial Dam LTVA outside of Yuma, AZ, includes a central facility with fresh water, dump station, trash, and coin-operated showers. The nearby independent Christian Center adds mail and package acceptance service, and fee-based services such as propane, salt-free water dispenser, and off-season trailer/rig storage.

Macerator – A device which grinds black waste to liquid and pumps it to the black tank. Used in RVs and trailers that do not have gravity flow to the black tank.

Mod – Slang for "modification," used in vanlife as a generic name for changes made to an existing DIY build or to customize a RV or camper van.

Off-grid – Ability to camp for a period of time without connecting to resources. Depending on their equipment and capacities, vanlifers can stay off-grid for a week or more without needing resource replenishment (typically water, waste-dumping, and propane). Usually off-grid-enabled vehicles use solar panels to recharge batteries, thus never need to connect to short power or drive to recharge, unless there is heavy cloud cover.

Overlander, overlanding – Type of vehicle and travel that is set up for more extreme terrain and locales. Overlanders enjoy the challenge of traveling and camping in places most regular vehicles cannot go. A philosophy of traveling in extreme wilderness to avoid organized camping areas and experience nature in a wild and undeveloped condition.

Pop-up – Ability in a camper van for the roof to pop up, typically to allow a sleeping platform in the raised area. Popularized in the 1960s in Volkswagen camper vans, pop-up roofs are a popular option on new RVs and camper vans outside the U.S. Inside the U.S., pop-ups are making a comeback from the '60s Volkswagon camper days as more RV manufacturers offer pop-ups in new Class B RVs and camper vans.

Potable or non-potable water – Important label to indicate whether water is safe to drink (potable), or unsafe to drink but usable to rinse out black tanks (non-potable or un-potable).

Propane / LPG – Fuel source common in camper vans, camping, and RVs. Typically provides inexpensive fuel source to power stoves and heaters, but older RVs and camper vans can also have propane-powered refrigerators. Safety is a concern when using propane inside a vehicle, and drivers who do should have a propane detector (along with carbon monoxide and smoke detectors), and open windows when cooking with propane. Tanks should be outside, or underneath the vehicle. If stored inside, they should be in a sealed box vented to the outside. Propane gas requires a regulator to control gas delivery.

Refilling is readily available at a variety of places, from specialized propane dealers to places like U-Haul, some campgrounds, some convenience stores and gas stations, etc. For vehicles with portable tanks, travelers can also swap for filled tanks at some grocery and hardware stores rather than use a propane refilling site.

Rig – Slang for a vehicle equipped as a camper van or RV, or even a DIY-converted passenger vehicle.

Road trip – Beloved phrase for those who love to drive and explore in a vehicle. Often used to define specific out-and-back travel.

Solar power – Energy source for recharging batteries powering RVs, vans, and camping vehicles. This is a recent trend that has become a standard feature on new RVs and camper vans. A solar panel collects energy via direct sunlight, then uses a solar controller to recharge the batteries that supply DC power to run lights, equipment, and appliances in a vehicle.

Stealth-camping – Overnighting at a place not commonly used for boondocking or camping, e.g., curbside in an industrial or multi-family residential area, big box store, restaurant, hospital, or other public locations. "Stealth" means minimizing attention. Achieved by using blackout curtains or window coverings to block seeing insight light and looking in from the outside. Staying overnight at a place depends on whether there are "no overnighting" signs or not, with vanlifers assuming if no sign posted against it, overnighting is okay. Common sense also plays a part in not being intrusive or disruptive to locals living in the area.

Vanlife, vandwelling – Coined term for the lifestyle of living in a van or appropriate vehicle.

Wild camping – see Boondocking.

APPENDIX B – RESOURCES & LINKS

From many years of travel, rig building, modding, and testing gear, I have explored a lot of equipment, parts, and resources for vanlife. This long list is not exhaustive, and may omit some great choices.

NOTE
The eBook version has clickable links for this section, but the print version does not. I have left the contents in this print version for you perusal.

You can download this Appendix as a separate PDF with clickable links at the URL below so you can easily access the resources and links.

https://BookHip.com/MBQGXQT

INFORMATION & RESOURCES

- Camping & Parks
- Domicile Residency
- Insurance
- Mail Services
- Memberships
- Roadside Assistance
- Smartphone Apps (Apple iOS)
- Social Media
- Solitude Reading List

PRODUCTS

- Accessories
- Camping
- Chassis & External Mods
- Comfort & Ventilation
- Connectivity
- Cooking & Kitchen
- Electronics & Gadgets
- Hiking & Nature
- Personal Hygiene
- Power & Solar
- Propane
- Travel
- Water & Waste

INFORMATION & RESOURCES

CAMPING & PARKS

BLM camping info and rules

BLM general info

Escapees

National Forest Service

National Parks Annual Pass (highly recommended, especially if 65 or older)

National Parks Service

Passport America

Recreation.gov

Thousand Trails

DOMICILE RESIDENCY

Deciding on which state you should use to establish your new domicile residency (if needed) is subjective to your situation. The Escapees links below provide good overall information on the process and details, but are subject to change if states revise their process or rules.

Florida – https://escapees.com/florida/

Texas – https://escapees.com/texas/

South Dakota – https://escapees.com/education/domicile/south-dakota/

INSURANCE

Progressive Insurance

RV insurance advice – https://escapees.com/7-things-you-need-to-know-about-rv-insurance/

RV insurance chart – https://money.com/best-rv-insurance/

MAIL SERVICES

Companies linked below provide mail forwarding service in the three states nomads typical use for domicile residency.

Florida

- **American Home Base** – http://www.amhomebase.com/
- **Good Sam** – https://www.goodsammailservice.com/
- **St. Brendan's Isle** (I used SBI – great service!) – https://www.sbimailservice.com/

Texas

- **Escapees** – https://www.escapees.com/support/mail-service
- **Texas Homebase** – http://texashomebase.com/
- **US Global Mail** – https://www.usglobalmail.com/

South Dakota

- **Dakota Post** – http://dakotapost.net/
- **Your Best Address** – http://www.yourbestaddress.com/

MEMBERSHIPS

Boondockers Welcome (now owned by Harvest Hosts)

Escapees

Harvest Hosts

ROADSIDE ASSISTANCE

Insurance based – Check with the insurer of your rig to learn if they offer roadside assistance coverage.

Comparisons – https://www.thervgeeks.com/best-rv-roadside-assistance/

SMARTPHONE APPS

Note: I use iPhone/iPad apps, but many of these are also available for Android. Links are to the Apple iPhone/iPad apps store.

All Stays – All around campground, parks, and services app. Been around a long time but is deep in locations and services

All Trails – GPS hiking and biking trail maps

Campendium – Campsites and boondocking locations

Drive Weather – Weather app, but with a twist: you can input all your stops along a route and see current and forecast weather for each stop

Free Roam – BLM & public land camping

Gaia GPS – Hiking, overlanding camping trail maps

GasBuddy – Gas price comparisons nearby or at a destination

Google Earth – Satellite view of terrain; handy for scoping out public camping areas in more detail

Hunting Points – GPS map showing ownership and viability of camping in wild areas

iHunter – Canada – Hunting app showing land ownership to determine rights to stay on land

iOverlander – Public campsites/grounds and overlooked public spots to camp for a night

RV Parks & Campgrounds – Search app for mostly paid camping sites

Parks Canada – Guide to Canadian parks

RV Dumpsites – Place an icon on your device with this link: rvdump-sites.net – use to find dump sites in cities and towns

Sanidumps USA – Another dump station finder; place icon on your device with this link: sanidumps.com

Site Locator US – Shows nearby cell towers if you need to align your campsite with them

Surfshark – Good, inexpensive VPN; a must (VPN) for connecting to any public Wi-Fi

Tower Locator – Another app to show Canadian cell tower locations

Trucker Path – Truck stops and weight stations

Truma – Useful app from the German heater maker for help in leveling your vehicle (in the app's tool section)

Ultimate Canadian Campground Project – Search app for Canadian campgrounds

Ultimate CG – Search app for US campgrounds

Walkmeter – Hiking/walking GPS tracking app; very helpful to track your stats and provides a visual map of the path you took to hike in that helps you follow to hike back out

SOCIAL MEDIA

Facebook Groups

These topic-specific resources are a great place to learn about vanlife, camping, RVs, etc. Search on Facebook for topics of interest then pick groups to explore.

Suggestions for choosing a good topic-related Facebook group:

- If you own or considering a manufacturer's RV (e.g., Winnebago Travato Class B, Thor Rize class B, Pleasureway, etc.), then find a group specific to that model.
- Look for groups with LOTS of members (the hive mind and broad experiences is where you want to be.
- Read the group description to make sure the group is likely to have the information you want
- Make sure the group has appropriate rules for good member behavior and a safe place to be.
- After joining, explore the Files section first. There may be guidelines and checklists to help you.
- Rather than immediately posting, spend time across several days (or more) to explore your questions using group search. Odds are your questions were answered before, probably many times.
- *If your interest is in lifestyle,* then similar suggestions apply, although put more importance on the description and group rules to see if the environment and topic coverage is what you want.
- *If your interest is in travel and travel tips,* loosely follow the above advice and spend time searching and exploring to gauge the quality of experiences and tips shared.

Other social media

Instagram is a great ongoing resource for other's experience, tips, and suggestions (and posting your own).

SOLITUDE READING LIST

This list of books are ones I've read and studied. There are certainly many more available, but I found these good and worth reading if interested in solitude, solitary life, or helping to understand loneliness.

- At the Center of All Beauty: Solitude and the Creative Life
- Celebrating Time Alone: Stories of Splendid Solitude
- Quiet: The Power of Introverts in a World That Can't Stop Talking
- Silence: In the Age of Noise
- Solitude: In Pursuit of a Singular Life in a Crowded World
- The Art of Solitude
- The Genius of Solitude: How to Be Alone Without Being Lonely

---

PRODUCTS

I have tried or used nearly every product listed (unless noted). *Most product listings are affiliate links* where I get a small commission that helps support my writings and small press publishing company.

ACCESSORIES

Buckles and strap, 1" – For securing many types of things (these straps are rigid, thus better than bungee-type straps)

Case, Pelican – For secret stash stuff

Cinch straps 1" x 12"

Door draft stopper, 48" cedar & pine filled

Folding stool, 11"

Folding stool, 9"

Ladder, 10.5' telescoping, 330# capacity

Leveler, Froli compact – 15% off through this link, plus check out my video review here

Leveler, Froli curved large – 15% off through this link (review is also on my YouTube channel but posted after this book's publication)

Magnetic Board 7.5" x 12"

Magnetic mirror 5" x 7"

Recovery treads, folding GoTreads

Safety cone, 17" collapsible – Useful in an emergency but also to show campsite occupied if you leave temporarily (some vanlifers buy a cheap camping tent and leave set up to show "occupied")

Sealant, adhesive for roof equipment – What Winnebago uses

Shoe organizer, mesh pocket – Fits behind van cab seats; minimal design and lightweight

Squeegee, compact w/3' extension pole – Cleaning solar panels or windows

Weatherstripping, 2" x 1/8" black foam – Rattles and cushioning

Whisk broom/dustpan

CAMPING

Chair, camping – Helionox-style

Chair, REI camping relaxing – This is my current camp chair and love it for comfort and affordability

Light, solar powered for camping

Shelter, Clam Explorer 6" x 6" w/3 windscreens

Table, medium side or low, two-person eating

CHASSIS & EXTERNAL MODS

Oil drain valve, Fumoto F-106 for Promasters

Oil drain valve, Fumoto F-106 cover accessory for Promasters

Ramps, Rhino MAX 16,000# capacity

Sound deadening sheets, KILMAT 80 mil. 36 s.f.

Tire pressure gauge, up to 60#

Tire pressure gauge, up to 100#

Tire repair/patch kit, Rhino USA

Trailer hitch pin & built-in clip, stainless steel Master Lock

Trailer hitch step, black Bully Bar (no lights)

Weatherseal, black rubber 5/16" x ¼" x 17' – For air/light gaps at doors

COMFORT & VENTILATION

Bed suspension system, Froli stars – Provides air flow underneath plus cushioning similar to individual mattress coils; use the link above to get 15% off

Curtains, blackout cab 63" length, 2 – 38" panels – Fits Promaster cabs

Fan, 12v clip

Fan, Caframo 12v Ultimate – Versatile to move around in vehicle

Fan, Caframo 12v Sirocco II – Just added this to the van and LOVE it. Pricey, but worth it for what it can do and how quiet it is (relative to all the other 12v fans I tried over the years)

CONNECTIVITY

Antenna, lift-and-fold adapter for OTR (or any stick type) antenna

Antenna, MiMO – For Wi-Fi hotspots with twin TS-9 connectors

Antenna, OTR roof extended

Cell boost, WeBoost Drive Reach – For RV, truck

Cell boost, WeBoost Sleek – For smartphones

COOKING & KITCHEN

Cooker, Hot Logic mini 12v

Cooktop, single burner induction – Currently my cooktop in my van; like that I can store this away when not needed, thus freeing up precious counter space for other uses

Cookware, induction cooktops – VAST majority of non-stick cookware surfaces are unhealthy (despite what their product blurbs would infer); link is to well-made, lightweight German non-stick pans that pass the (current) test of not having the nasty chemicals used in most non-stick pots and pans

Grill, campfire stainless – Most campsite campfire cooking grates are not so clean; this takes the worry out of that by carrying your own, clean grate to use

Hammock, fruit & veggies, two hooks – Macrame under cabinet hanging

Hammock, fruit & veggies two hanging bars – Macrame under-cabinet hanging

Measuring cups, camping

Mug, GSI outdoor

Storage, 2-tier rotating trays, 9" round

Storage, container bins, two-pack

Storage, loose tea or coffee – Stainless steel 550ml

Storage, rectangular small bins 6" x 3" x 2" – Good to hang on wall or drawer storage

Storage, Rubbermaid lettuce container – 11.1 cup, square

Stove, dual burner propane camp stove

Stove, fast boil, Fire-Maple – JetBoil clone, as good, much cheaper

Stove, single burner camp stove GasOne – Propane or butane

Teakettle, electric 110v – 0.8 liter, black

Teakettle, gooseneck stovetop – 1 liter

ELECTRONICS & GADGETS

Air compressor, Viair 400P

GPS unit, Garmin RV 770

GPS unit, sun shade – For 7" GPS units

Hand warmer, OCOOPA 10,000mAh – Great gadget for cold weather USB rechargeable

Headlamp, 1100 lumens – 2-pack

Multimeter, Innova 3320 – Necessary for 12v electrical work

OBD scanner – OBDLink MX+ bluetooth scanner

Phone mount – 360 rotation dashboard

Phone mount – Cup holder

Phone mount – Dash/windshield

Printer, HP LaserJet M110W – Monochrome, smallest true laser printer available

Reading light – 12v bedside reading light

Reading light – 12v gooseneck bed light

Selfie stick smartphone tripod with wireless remote

Tablet mount, ceiling

Tool, wire crimper

Tool, auto wire stripper

USB outlet – Two type A

USB outlet – Two type C, one type A

Wire, crimp connection kit

Wire, heat-shrink sleeves

Weather station, three sensors, atomic clock

HIKING & NATURE

Backpack, eyeglasses strap holder

Backpack, Osprey lightweight

Backpack, smartphone strap holder

Camera harness, chest – Safest way to hike with a SLR/DLR camera

Chair, Coleman event stool – Backpack portable

GPS emergency/text device, Garmin InReach

GPS emergency/text device, InReach backpack tether holster

Hat, hiking – Tilley

Poles, trekking Black Diamond pair

Water storage bottle Nalgene Tritan – Wide mount 480z

Water storage bottle, Camelbak internal straw

Water storage bottle pouch for Camelbak – Excellent to walk/light hike with if not carrying a backpack; I use this a lot

PERSONAL HYGIENE

Bucket, collapsible with lid

Shower, camping hand-held electric pump

Shower, hanging solar 2.5 gallon – 3 or 5 gallon also available, but heavy when filled

Shower, portable kit

Shower, non-slip silicone folding mat

Laundry, collapsible hamper

Toilet, Stansport portable 14" x 14" x 14"

POWER & SOLAR

Inverter, Xantrex 2kw true sinewave

Inverter, Xantrex remote control switch

Inverter, Xantrex transfer switch

Solar generator, portable panels – Jackery

PROPANE

Mopeka, tank halo – Shim for Winnebago Solis Pocket or any other rig with propane bottles to allow tank monitor to function

Tank monitor, bluetooth

TRAVEL

Maps, Benchmark – Arizona

Maps, Benchmark – California

Maps, Benchmark – Colorado

Maps, Benchmark – New Mexico

Maps, Benchmark – Oregon

Maps, Benchmark – Utah

WATER & WASTE

Filter, Camco TastePure

Hose, Camco 90-degree elbow fitting

Hose, Camco flexible hose protector with gripper

Hose, Zero-G flexible safe for drinking water 25′

Regulator, water, Camco stainless steel

Sewer cap, Camco with flange – For easier opening and small hose outlet

Sewer hose, Valterra 10′ plus clear angle adapter

Sewer tank treatment, Happy Camper organic – 18 treatments

Water tap, Camco water bandit – For taps with stripped or no threads

Water, Valterra blow-out plug – For safely winterizing water pipes and fittings using small compressor

Water, USB rechargable pump – For 3- or 5-gallon water jugs

APPENDIX C – MORE OF MY STORY

> Nothing behind me, everything ahead of me, as is ever so on the road.
>
> JACK KEROUAC

BACKSTORY

I am a baby boomer. I say that humbly, realizing it reveals two things about me: my general age, and my formative experiences during the '50s, '60s, and '70s.

To say I have lived a varied life would be true, but not tell the full story. My list of interests, jobs, pursuits, and failed dreams are quite long, but I will not share them here. You are welcome for that kindness!

It is fair to say two things were constant from adolescence to where I am today: a love of nature, and a soul determined to breathe in and enjoy the intoxicating air of wanderlust. Bound by the usual cultural and economic constraints up until I retired from the corporate world, I chased this elusive muse when and where I could, which translates to "not often enough." Yet, in those times of travel and nature immersion, I knew I was on to something. In a mental exercise of what I might tell my younger self, it would be to eschew the trappings of consumerism and the delaying tactics of working for someone else, and at an early age hit the road, or trail, or wild pastures often.

Yet, I have no regrets. My varied jobs and interests, and what time I did spend traveling and in nature, all brought me to where I am today: a modern nomad exploring what is outside my van's windows and inside myself.

My later years of work consisted of various efforts along a roughly creative path, from video production to technical writing to corporate narrative, and in the years within the shadow of retirement: corporate communications. Those last years of corporate life set me up financially to travel, explore nature, and write on the road.

I committed to my first year of full-time vanlife by researching what to buy and how to live, following much of the ideas and guidance I have included in this book. Although experienced with hiking and camping, living in a vehicle while traveling was not familiar to me.

MY VANLIFE SOLUTIONS

My first van was Winnebago Travato K, a Class B RV, which I named Tamasté. Much like boat owners, vanlifers often name their vans or RVs. Tamasté came equipped with the creature comforts I thought I needed and wanted. Many of those continue in my current van, but I learned early in my Travato travels that some were unnecessary for me.

I sold that RV shortly before the COVID-19 pandemic arrived. I had selected Tamasté's replacement and placed a deposit on a Pleasureway Tofino, a modern van owing roots to the '60s Volkswagen camper vans, but I cancelled before delivery, when the pandemic grounded us all.

I decided if I could not travel, I would temporarily open an online stationery store (stationery being yet another passion). Notegeist, the third such store over a five-year period, kept me busy and distracted during 2020, providing virtual contact with so many other kindred spirits (aka, stationery nerds).

Throughout 2020, I continued research for my next van, undecided between buying an empty cargo van and doing my own custom conversion, or getting another production camper van. Although I had several major trips planned outside the U.S., I realized for the foreseeable future the only sane and safe way to travel was inside a van, where I could control my COVID-19 exposure risk by being self-contained for food, sleep, and bathroom needs.

By the end of 2020, I began to see light shining through a slowly opening window where vanlife might be possible again. I closed Notegeist and began in earnest to look for a van that would work for me. Still unsure exactly which, I began to explore an alternate vehicle type I could travel part-time in.

On YouTube I found Chase Christopher who converted his Subaru Outback into a camper of sorts. That intrigued me, so I traded my beloved Subaru Crosstrek in for a new Outback. I built my version of his Subaru Outback camper layout and began a six-to-eight week experimental trip during the summer of 2021. While I loved how the layout worked, I quickly realized it was a great solution for a week now and then, or if I was a twenty-something! For me, it was not a good solution for extended traveling.

During that trip in the Outback, on my way from Colorado back home to Michigan, I stopped off in Iowa to visit my Travato dealer, Lichtsinn RV. I knew I wanted to check out and drive Winnebago's pop-top Solis. Winnebago had also just announced a newer variant, the Solis Pocket, which is even shorter and simpler than the regular Solis. Having seen the promo videos, I was somewhat interested in looking at it, but mostly wanted to see the larger Solis with pop-top roof.

As it turns out, I never drove, or even went inside a pop-top Solis! Looking at the Solis Pocket when I arrived, it was a classic of moment of love at first sight. Test driving confirmed what I hoped to feel with a much shorter van: easy to drive, turn, and park. The layout was similar to what I had sketched out for my own van build, and close to my overall vision. Plus the Pocket could be ready soon, not take a year to build. There were still modifications I would want to get the features I envisioned in a custom build-out, but the benefits of having most of my list and needs available immediately was compelling.

In late September of 2021, I drove to Lichtsinn RV in Forest City, Iowa, to trade in my Subaru Outback (now without the camper conversion and reverted to its original state), which was crammed full of everything I needed to hit the road in the Pocket. From there, I would drive my new van through the Dakotas, Colorado, the Southwest, then over to California for a drive up the western coast of the U.S. Finally, I drove back to Arizona to spend the winter at a long-term visitor area near Yuma, Arizona.

As I write these words, I am back home in Michigan after that long trip. During the last two months I have completed Phase 2 of planned improvements to VanGeist, my Solis Pocket. This effort brings VanGeist closer to the ideal van that I envision for myself.

There is one last, fantasy step to reach my ideal van, a radical effort requiring significant funding: a fully self-sustained van running on only gasoline, solar, and water. Phase 3 would double my lithium batteries (I upgraded to two lithiums out in California); remove the propane system, including the cooktop and the Truma heating system, and replace them with an induction cooktop and a Webasto gasoline-fueled heater. Whether this magic ever takes place is uncertain.

The upgrades I have made from the stock Soils Pocket have certainly turned VanGeist into a fantastic solo-traveler van. My upgrades include two lithium batteries, 2kw inverter, AT tires, Sumo springs, underneath spare tire, and much, much more.

THE ROAD STILL CALLS ME

A few short weeks from now, I will head out for another phase of extensive travel, into New England and some of Canada, followed by more time exploring my own backyard of Michigan's Upper Peninsula.

If you are out there traveling and enjoying the vanlife, or traveling and dreaming of vanlife one day, if you see my white VanGeist in a campground, the wild, or an overnight parking lot, be sure to say hello!

May your travels be often, your time in nature serene, and your quest to find the inner contentment that comes with vanlife be successful.

See you on down the road!

APPENDIX D –
CONTACT & FOLLOW

Follow my vlog on travels and vanlife stuff at my YouTube channel, **Adventures Nomadic**. There you can also watch the dozen or so videos I produced during my Subaru Outback camper conversion experiment. *Be sure to subscribe to the channel so you get notices when I post new videos.*

Follow my blog posts at **garyvarner.com** on journeys, vanlife, and other stuff. Be sure to subscribe to email notifications when I publish new posts.

Send me a message via **my site's contact form**, should you wish to ask a question, comment on this book, or just say hello.

Finally, check my Instagram feed **@inkmuser** for photos, humor, and other bits about life.

Thanks for reading *Modern Nomad: The Vanlife Alternative.*

I hope my efforts to share this information encourages you to get out there, explore the world, and get to know yourself better.

www.ingramcontent.com/pod-product-compliance
Lightning Source LLC
Chambersburg PA
CBHW071855020426
42331CB00010B/2528